T0267212

TRUE CRIME STORIES
OF THE
TRIAD

CATHY PICKENS

THE
History
PRESS

Published by The History Press
Charleston, SC
www.historypress.com

First published 2024

Manufactured in the United States

ISBN 9781467156714

Library of Congress Control Number: 2024941837

Notice: The information in this book is true and complete to the best of our knowledge. It is offered without guarantee on the part of the author or The History Press. The author and The History Press disclaim all liability in connection with the use of this book.

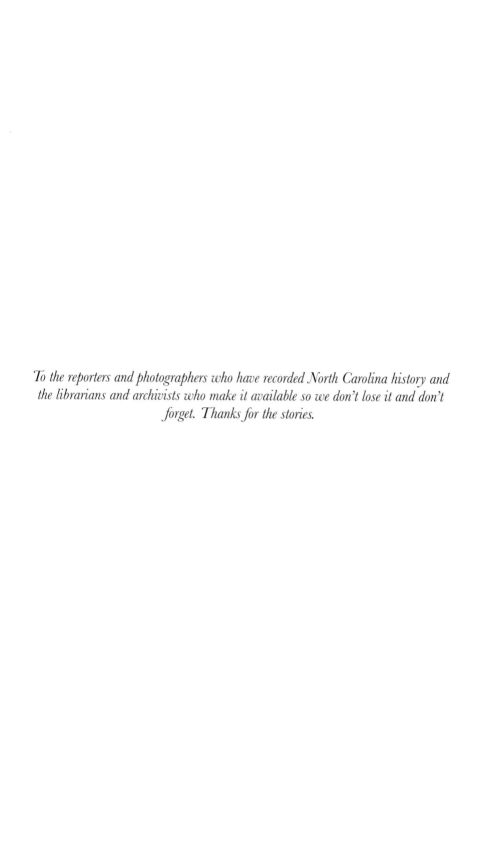

To the reporters and photographers who have recorded North Carolina history and the librarians and archivists who make it available so we don't lose it and don't forget. Thanks for the stories.

CONTENTS

ACKNOWLEDGEMENTS

MANY THANKS TO THOSE who've contributed their expertise to this book:

Luci Zahray, The Poison Lady, who clarified how one might *not* die from arsenic

Beverly Wiggins, volunteer at Chatham County Historical Association

Kate Jenkins, Jonny Foster, Abigail Fleming and the rest of the amazing team at The History Press

Paula Connolly and her constant friendship and storyteller's eye

E. Dickinson, scary-good at catching errors and taking photographs

As always, to Bob, who is along for every adventure.

TRIAD CRIME SCENES

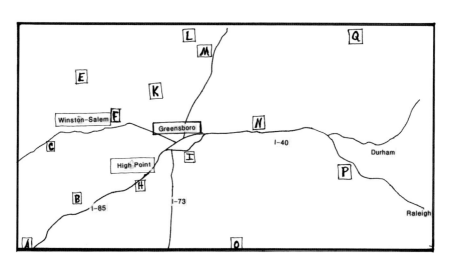

A	Salisbury	K	Summerfield
B	Lexington	L	Wentworth
C	Clemmons	M	Reidsville
	Winston-Salem	N	Burlington
E	Germanton	O	Chatham County
F	Kernersville	P	Chapel Hill
	High Point	Q	Roxboro
H	Trinity		Durham
I	Pleasant Garden		Raleigh
	Greensboro		

WELCOME

The Triad area of North Carolina sits in the state's Piedmont region, identified by its trio of central cities: Greensboro, Winston-Salem and High Point. Once a farming area crossed by major trading paths and later railroads, the Triad became home to major tobacco, textile and furniture manufacturing companies—and the wealth those created. Names like Hanes and Burlington textiles, R.J. Reynolds and Lorillard tobacco, Lexington and Thomasville furniture graced office buildings and manufacturing plants around the region that employed thousands of workers. Though some operations have shrunk in size, their influence is still evident.

The Triad also boasts colleges and universities: the University of North Carolina–Greensboro and Wake Forest University, along with their research and innovation facilities; North Carolina A&T University; Elon University; High Point University; and Salem College, among others.

And the area's food innovators provide tasty treats of all kinds: Krispy Kreme Doughnuts, K&W Cafeterias and Texas Pete are all headquartered in Winston-Salem; Cook Out fast-food restaurants started in Greensboro.

Located conveniently between the western North Carolina mountains and the Outer Banks and coastal regions, the Triad has it all—including plenty of interesting crime stories. As recently as 2018, six North Carolina cities made it onto the FBI's list of deadliest cities, measured by murder rate per 100,000 residents. More than half of the cities on the FBI's list are in the South. North Carolina had more of the sixty-five cities than any other state—and the Triad had more than any other region in the state:

The Carolina Theater in downtown Greensboro first opened on Halloween night in 1927. *Courtesy of Elijah Mears via Unsplash.*

No. 25 High Point (16.09 murders per 100,000 residents)
No. 39 Greensboro (12.9)
No. 56 Winston-Salem (12.5)

Rounding out the North Carolina cities were Durham (no. 52), Fayetteville (no. 55) and Charlotte (no. 59). South Carolina boasted only two cities on the list, but both of those recorded more murders per capita than any of the North Carolina cities—Columbia (no. 17) and North Charleston (no. 14). As a comparison, Chicago—traditionally a city with a high murder rate—ranked no. 28 (18.26 murders per 100,000). St. Louis, Missouri, was no. 1 (with a startling 65.54 murders).

The South has historically been a deadly place, so the region's high ranking in the national murder statistics is no surprise. Statistics show that, without the South, the nation's murder rate would more closely resemble the lower rates in other wealthy, progressive countries. According to historian Roger Lane in *Murder in America: A History*, "The whole American scandalously high homicide rates are Southern in origin." The reasons incite lively debate, but the explanations offered don't really explain much.

Murder rates ebb and flow, and the rankings vary widely from year to year, sometimes for reasons not easily discerned. Numbers don't paint the full picture, and crime stories are always more interesting than statistics. These Triad-based cases cover several decades of murder and mayhem, with deadly family sagas, a colorful gang of high-class home-break-in artists, the state's first murder conviction without a body and a uniquely high number of female serial poisoners. The crimes happen in small towns, rural farmhouses and elegant mansions, carried out by criminals who were just visiting, some who were born in the Triad but moved elsewhere and plenty who stayed close to home.

History and its stories shape a region and the people who live there, in ways subtle and surprising and unavoidable. My family has been in the Carolinas more than three hundred years, steeped in Southern storytelling. Because any retelling of stories naturally depends on the storyteller's choices, these stories are those that, for one reason or another, captured my imagination.

This book is not a work of investigative journalism. The information is drawn solely from published or broadcast resources, including newspapers,

Winston-Salem skyline with R.J. Reynolds stacks and the Winston tower. *Courtesy of Ian McIlwraith via Unsplash.*

11

Celebrating the region's furniture industry, the World's Largest Chest of Drawers sits on High Point's North Hamilton Street. *Courtesy of Cmalaspina via Wikimedia Commons.*

television documentaries, podcasts, books, print and online magazine articles, appellate court decisions and scholarly papers.

One of the handicaps in recounting historical events is that accounts vary. Some reported "facts" aren't accurate—or are at odds with someone else's memory or perception of the event. While I have worked to dig out as many points of view as I could find, I'm sure there are mistakes. My apologies in advance.

For me, what fascinates is not random violence but people and their lives. Some of these stories could have happened anywhere. Some made huge headlines far away from the North Carolina Piedmont. Others remain writ large mostly in the hearts of family and friends of those involved.

All of them, woven together, demonstrate the rich variety of those who call this part of the state home, the importance of family and friends, the contrasts in modern cities nestled among small towns. People and their stories matter here. The stories are worth remembering, even when they involved loss and especially when they are tempered with respect.

Welcome to the Triad region of North Carolina and its crime stories.

1
THE POISONERS

NANNIE DOSS, THE GIGGLING GRANDMA

Between November 4, 1905, when she was born in Alabama, and when she eventually finished her life in an Oklahoma prison, Nannie Doss lived for less than three years in Lexington, North Carolina, with her third husband, Arlie Lanning. She met him in her favorite source for new husbands: a romance magazine's lonely-hearts column. They'd corresponded for months and married days after she stepped off the bus in Lexington. When Arlie died of a supposed heart attack in 1952, he bequeathed to his sister the house where he and Nannie lived. But the fire insurance policy was in Nannie's name, so when the house burned down, the $1,475 insurance proceeds went to Nannie as his executor and left his sister the poorer for it (about $18,000 today).

For three decades, the cheerful, giggling Nannie Doss (born Nancy Hazel) traveled the country. Along the way, she poisoned an estimated eleven family members, including four husbands (Arlie among them), her mother and her grandson. She was the first of the modern-day female serial poisoners to call North Carolina home, almost a textbook profile of such killers and, at the same time, one of the most colorful.

An unfathomable oddity about female serial poisoners is that they commit such terrible acts for such piddling rewards. The typical profile is a woman not born into the easiest circumstances; poverty and abuse are common in their backgrounds. They use poison as a sneaky and often effective means to avoid difficult or abusive situations. They poison family members almost exclusively, though sometimes they include vulnerable children or elderly victims for whom they serve as caregivers. And they kill for little or no financial gain, small insurance payments at best.

Rat poison—cheap, easy to come by and usually containing deadly effective arsenic—seemed Nannie's poison of choice. As the years passed, if anyone asked questions or voiced any concerns about Nannie's string of unfortunate family losses, it was done in private, not on the public record. She didn't tend to stay in one place, which helped hide how many of her loved ones had died mysterious and sudden deaths.

Nannie found her husbands through lonely-hearts columns and correspondence clubs, the precursor of online dating. In interviews, Nannie said she never killed for money, even though she did collect on some life insurance policies, ranging from $500 to $1,200. Her true goal, she confessed, was finding true love, "the perfect mate, the real romance of life," just like she read about in her romance magazines. Unfortunately, too many of the husbands turned out to be bad to drink or quick to run around with other women. When her real-life husbands fell short of the romantic ideal she avidly read about or when a family member got in the way, she found an easy escape—easy for her to carry out, though tormenting for her victims.

After factory worker Arlie died in Lexington, she married husband number four in Kansas. Her new husband's mother soon moved in with them—and almost as quickly, she died. Husband number four joined his mother in a Kansas graveyard three months later, and Nannie—known to some as the Jolly Widow—was back to perusing the lonely-hearts ads.

Husband number five, God-fearing Samuel Doss, married her in Tulsa, Oklahoma, in June 1953. Unfortunately for the former truck driver, he was a bit too straight and narrow and frowned on Nannie's romance-reading pastime. By October, he was dead of what doctors initially diagnosed as a gastric infection. The doctors were suspicious enough to investigate his illness and quick death, and they found a significant quantity of arsenic in his body. Turns out he loved stewed prunes, and Nannie obliged him with a big bowl shortly before he fell ill.

Nannie was arrested in Oklahoma after Samuel Doss's death. Her first husband, the one she'd met while working in a textile mill and married when she was only fifteen or sixteen, was the only one who survived marrying her. In interviews after her arrest, Charlie said two of their four daughters died of food poisoning soon after breakfast. He said he left and took up with another woman because Nannie scared him.

Investigators from Kansas, Oklahoma and North Carolina—places Nannie had lived—began comparing notes and exhuming bodies. According to UK journalist Terry Manners, the toxicologist at Duke University found Arlie Lanning was "saturated in arsenic" and said he "must have been in a lot of pain."

When the news of Nannie's arrest broke, those who'd known her during the years she lived in Davidson County in North Carolina described her, according to the Winston-Salem newspaper, as a "quiet woman whom nobody really knew."

Before she was arrested, Nannie was apparently planning to return to North Carolina. She was corresponding with a dairy farmer in Goldsboro who told the *Daily Oklahoman* that he was now "through with all these women who make their matches by mail."

Nannie confessed to Oklahoma investigators that she'd poisoned her husbands—"dullards," she called them. As more bodies of those who'd died in her proximity were exhumed and tested for arsenic, she became quite a media darling, with her close-cut bouncy curls, her beaming smile, her girlish giggle and her well-padded, grandmotherly figure. She generously gave interviews and charmed those around her.

Her Tulsa trial was set to begin June 2, 1955, but in May, she surprised law enforcement by pleading guilty. She avoided the death penalty and was sentenced to life in prison. In 1964, after Nannie was denied clemency, Manners reported her sentiments: "Sometimes I wish the authorities would let me be tried in North Carolina. Maybe they would give me the electric chair. Time passes slowly in prison. Behind my smile is a heavy heart. I have always made people think I was happy, even though I wasn't."

Nannie loved to cook and repeatedly applied during her incarceration to work in the prison kitchen. Not surprisingly, officials denied her requests.

While held in McAlester, Oklahoma, she stopped giving interviews. She didn't want to say anything to endanger any chance she had at parole. Few news reports mentioned the fact that she had four murder charges pending against her in other states—one each in Kansas and Alabama, and two in North Carolina for the deaths of husband Arlie Lanning in 1952 and of her mother, Louisa Hazel, in 1953. The Winston-Salem news editor noted that her mother's murder was the only one she denied committing.

Lexington's historic Davidson County Courthouse, photographed in 1940, was in use when Nannie Doss's murders were uncovered. *Courtesy of Frederick D. Nichols, Historic American Buildings Survey via Wikimedia Commons.*

Her parole never happened, and she never faced trials in those other deaths. Nannie remained in Oklahoma's women's prison until she died of leukemia in 1965 at age fifty-nine—ten years exactly after she was sentenced to prison.

REBECCA DETTER: HELPFUL HITMEN ARE HARD TO FIND

On June 10, 1977, the simple obituary for Don Gene Detter, age thirty-nine, in the *Winston-Salem Journal* identified him as a Wofford College graduate and an insurance agent for Reserve Life. He was survived by his wife, Rebecca, two sons and a daughter. As with most obituaries, it gave the facts but so little of the story.

On June 7, Don Detter had been admitted for the second time in four months to Forsyth Memorial Hospital. This time, he was in critical condition and died three days later. Using samples of his blood, urine and hair taken at his autopsy, tests at the toxicology lab in Chapel Hill—which took some time to process in the late 1970s—showed high levels of arsenic.

In January 1978, seven months after his death, the newspaper announced that a Forsyth County grand jury had handed down the first-degree murder indictment of Rebecca Detter, age thirty-six, of Kernersville. She'd been arrested two months earlier, in November.

This was big news in Kernersville and Forsyth County, and newspapers covered every step of the legal proceedings. As the case unfolded in court hearings and newspaper articles, it became clear that Joan Brooks—a seventeen-year-old friend of the Detters' son Ted—was a critical witness in the case.

Before Don Detter became ill, Joan Brooks became a regular visitor at the Detters' home. She heard from Rebecca how "cruel" husband Don was to the family, but Joan knew Don as a man who was "always joking, always carrying on a conversation, talking to you." That was, until he returned from a weeks-long hospital stay in March or April. When he came home, Joan said, he was weak and pale and "didn't have very much to say at all."

Sometime in February, before that first hospital stay, Joan Brooks said she'd run an errand for Mrs. Detter to Kernersville's Crown Drug Store to buy ant poison. February was also the time Don began seeing a physician complaining of flu-like symptoms and numbness in his fingers and toes.

During Don's hospital stay in February, his doctor said they found no sign of heavy metals in his urine. Instead, they linked his illness to his heavy drinking—Don admitted he daily drank about six beers, plus two fifths of liquor each week. Dr. William Spencer testified that Don was sent home with instructions to rest, relax and cut back on his alcohol consumption. Dr. Spencer wasn't convinced that Don's problem stemmed from his drinking, but at the time, he didn't have evidence of anything else.

Crown Drug Stores was a regional chain founded in Winston-Salem in 1964, when it introduced this logo. *Courtesy of Logopedia via Creative Commons.*

When investigators later began looking into how Don could have ingested arsenic, teenaged Joan told them that she saw Rebecca Detter pour three or four capfuls of Terro Ant Killer into Don's food, ice cream and iced tea—to sweeten it, Rebecca had explained to Joan.

Liquid ant poison is sweet, which attracts ants. At the time, Terro Ant Killer included the active ingredient sodium arsenate, which explains why Terro was also the favorite food additive and murder weapon of Velma Barfield, another of North Carolina's most notorious arsenic poisoners.

Joan Brooks said that after another drugstore trip, Rebecca asked her to take the boxes from two bottles of ant killer and "throw them out of her car window when she went home." Even though she had witnessed incidents that led up to Don's death, she did as her friend's mother asked. And she kept returning to the Detters' house because Rebecca kept inviting her. Joan said she was scared not to go, that she "didn't think she would have second thoughts about trying to do something to me."

Prosecutors aren't required to produce evidence of motive, but the "why" of a murder is always a key question for jurors and court watchers. Joan Brooks could provide some hint of motive: Don Detter refused to give Rebecca a divorce, she said.

Pending trial, Rebecca was released from jail on a $27,500 bond (about $75,000 today). The death penalty, as applied by the states, had been held unconstitutional in a 1972 U.S. Supreme Court decision. North Carolina adopted a new statute on June 1, 1977, which meant Rebecca Detter could face the death penalty.

At trial, nineteen-year-old Joan Brooks was the state's first and most damaging witness. In addition to involving Joan in the poisoning, Rebecca also told her that she'd tampered with the brakes on Don's car. Why Rebecca Detter felt so confident about letting a teenager into her murderous plot was never clear. But, after Don Detter died, Rebecca threatened Joan: "She told me I was the only one who could hurt her, and I'd better keep my mouth shut." Joan had tears in her eyes as she revealed that information to the jury.

Was Joan's testimony—or that of other witnesses—coerced or threatened from them by the prosecutor? At trial, the defense attorney pressed several witnesses on that point during cross-examination, especially Joan Brooks. Had the prosecutor told her that she too could be hauled into court as a defendant? Yes, she said, he'd said she could be indicted, but he said that only after she'd told her story to the investigators, not before.

Joan Brooks wasn't the only witness that explained how busy Rebecca Detter had been in the days and weeks before her husband's hospitalization and death. In January 1977, Rebecca motioned a school bus driver over to her white Cadillac while both were parked outside the junior high school. She knew the bus driver casually; they'd met at a party. She asked if he'd kill her husband for $5,000. When he refused her offer, she asked if he knew where she could get some "lead arsenic" (more accurately, lead arsenate, commonly used in insecticides)—and if he thought that would kill him, as if the bus driver might have an expert opinion. He testified, "I thought she was crazy for what she was doing," and said he told her to just leave her husband and get a divorce.

Rebecca also asked her longtime hairdresser—whose husband used "dope"—if they could get her some drugs. She wanted to kill her husband. The hairdresser didn't help out with the drugs, and she didn't provide investigators with the fake alibi Rebecca needed, either. Rebecca wanted to claim she'd been at the salon the night Don Detter died, when she was really with a man named "Gene," reportedly a preacher from Baltimore. Rebecca said Gene was her children's godfather, but many suspected he was the other man in her life.

Her friends weren't helping out, so Rebecca contacted a known drug dealer, offering him her going rate of $5,000 for a hit on her husband. When he said no, she asked for drugs that would kill him. Over the next two months, she paid him $250 for doses of cocaine, LSD and PCP, known as angel dust, and later complained about his bad customer service because her husband was still alive. She had added the drugs to Don's favorite egg salad, but it only made him "happy." She asked the drug dealer if he could he get her some DDT (an insecticide used as a mosquito spray until its ban in 1972). No, he couldn't. Could he use a syringe and inject some air in her husband's veins and kill him? No, he wouldn't.

At trial, the admitted former drug dealer and heavy drug user testified that he didn't give Rebecca full value for her $250. He used some of her money to buy drugs for himself and cut the drugs he gave her to weaken them. "I knew myself that it wouldn't kill the man."

Don had been released from his first visit at Forsyth Memorial Hospital on April 13. He returned to the emergency room on May 17. At trial, one of his doctors testified that they knew the day after his second admission that he'd been poisoned with arsenic. The numbness in his extremities had worsened and he could hardly move. He was vomiting and had lost weight. The doctors also observed telltale Mees' lines on his fingernails—white lines that grow out with the nail and can indicate kidney failure or long-term heavy metals poisoning. This time, the toxicology tests they ran revealed arsenic. Doctors tried to flush the poison from his system, but he remained in a coma for two weeks before he died.

Arsenic occurs naturally in the environment, and most humans will register low levels of the heavy metal if tested. But Dr. Arthur J. McBay, the chief toxicologist at the state medical examiner's lab, found ten milligrams of arsenic in Don's liver, a level ten times higher than normal. Dr. McBay testified that a one-ounce bottle of Terro Ant Killer would be lethal.

Rebecca Detter was the first witness her lawyers called to the stand during the defense's case. She denied everything anyone had said against her: she hadn't tried to hire anyone to kill her husband, she never bought any ant killer and she never tried to kill her husband. She said Don's drinking had a bad effect on their marriage, especially in the last four years after he was demoted to a sales job from a manager's position. She testified that he'd had twelve jobs during their nineteen-year marriage and he'd been fired from half of those. However, she said, "I was not dissatisfied with my husband."

Her September 1978 trial took six days. The jury deliberated for only one hour before finding her guilty of first-degree murder. She took the verdict without reaction. However, when officers walked to the back of the courtroom where her three children sat, she started crying as they arrested her eighteen-year-old son Ted, charging him with conspiracy in the murder. He later pleaded no contest and received a suspended sentence.

In the penalty phase, she was sentenced to death.

Rebecca's death sentence made new law for North Carolina. In its analysis of her appeal, the state's supreme court went into detail on whether certain evidence should have been admitted and found no basis for overturning the verdict. However, the court set aside the death penalty because, as her defense lawyer argued, the death penalty was "designed to punish acts, not results." Don Detter died on June 1, a week after the state's new statute went into effect. Rebecca's acts of administering poison all happened before that date. Her new mandatory sentence was life in prison.

In 1983, five years after her conviction, those who knew Rebecca Detter as a sweet, churchgoing lady and loving mother began petitioning Governor James Hunt to commute her sentence. At the same time, those intimately familiar with the family dynamic began talking

Bottle of vintage Terro Ant Killer, active ingredient: sodium arsenate. *From the author's collection; photo courtesy of E. Dickinson.*

publicly. One of her sons explained to Raleigh reporter Donald Patterson that his dad was a "good dude" until he started drinking. Then he would knock them around, throw stuff and rage when things didn't go his way. Once, when Ted refused to play a game of chess with him, Don "threatened to rebreak the arm I had hurt playing football." Finally, one night, Ted and his brother fought back, after which Don turned all his threats and violence toward their mother, Rebecca.

Ted recalled the night he watched his father threaten his mother with a rifle. Ted was hiding in the hallway outside his parents' bedroom holding another rifle in his hands, on alert. "You ain't worth shooting," Don told Rebecca as he lowered his weapon. Ted saw that his father's gun was missing its bolt; he couldn't have fired it. Ted always wondered what would've happened if he'd shot Don that night. Would he have had to serve any time, or would a jury have acquitted him based on self-defense? If he'd had to do time, he said, "I'd rather it be me than Momma."

Years after the turmoil at home, Ted also talked about why Rebecca didn't just leave. "She was scared to stay and scared to leave. She was staying in a living hell, that's all it was." While Battered Spouse Syndrome (BSS) remains a controversial defense, using it in a self-defense claim was only starting to be part of the conversation in legal circles in the 1970s. The first significant study of the post-traumatic effects on a battered spouse weren't published until 1976, in Dr. Lenore Walker's book, *The Battered Woman*. Over the following four decades, the legal conversation has continued to shift. The violence Ted Detter described as his father's circumstances deteriorated and he began to drink more steadily might have been treated differently in the courts—and perhaps Rebecca would have seen other, less drastic avenues of aid or escape.

In 1983, though, when Rebecca's push for clemency began in earnest, District Attorney Donald Tisdale didn't see the case the same way Rebecca's family and friends did. He regarded Don's death as one of "the most cold-blooded, calculated and heinous murders" he'd prosecuted. Investigating sheriff's deputy Bobby Joe Grindstaff joined Tisdale in opposing her early release. Descriptions of Don's forty-pound weight loss, the paralysis in his arms and legs, his raging 105-degree temperature as he struggled to breathe his last breaths while, according to one witness, she offered him sips of tea laced with arsenic—the reality of that horror was impressed on the law enforcement officials.

Meanwhile, Ted maintained the family home, painting and repairing it as best he could, waiting for the time when his mother could come home.

By December 1990, Rebecca was being held in minimum custody and on work release from the women's prison in Raleigh. According to North Carolina inmate records, she was released following parole in January 1997 after serving less than twenty years. The release caused no fanfare.

Why is Rebecca Detter not as well-known as other female North Carolina arsenic poisoners? Perhaps because she had only a single victim, though she was singularly determined to kill him. Given her chats with assorted potential accomplices, she also seemed recklessly nonchalant about who knew what she was plotting and carrying out.

North Carolina reinstated the death penalty in 1977 and currently has 135 men and 2 women on death row—Forsyth County sent 12 of those, the highest number of any county. But the state conducted no executions between 1962 and 1984; the last execution to date was in 2006.

BLANCHE TAYLOR MOORE, THE MINISTERING ANGEL

On February 17, 2023, Blanche Taylor Moore turned ninety years old. Convicted in Forsyth County, she was the oldest woman on death row in the United States—an honor she'd held for years. While in prison, she had undergone chemotherapy and radiation and survived cancer. Odds are she will bypass her death sentence and die a natural death in the North Carolina Correctional Institution for Women in Raleigh as one of the nation's most infamous serial poisoners.

In 1989, Blanche's second husband, the Reverend Dwight Moore, was deathly ill and hospitalized at the University of North Carolina in Chapel Hill. Doctors ran all manner of tests to identify the cause of his symptoms while working to save his life. Lab tests can be quick—but only if the lab knows what to look for. Heavy metals poisoning is rarely the first thing doctors expect when a patient presents with severe gastric distress. When they found that Reverend Moore had twenty times the normal level of arsenic, they immediately called the State Bureau of Investigation (SBI).

Investigators came to the hospital to question Reverend Moore, and he mentioned that Blanche's former boyfriend Raymond Reid had died of Guillain-Barré syndrome. Coincidentally, both Guillain-Barré and arsenic poisoning can present with severe gastroenteritis and progressive neuropathy.

Doctors and investigators pulled Raymond Reid's medical records. In May 1986, he was admitted to the hospital in Greensboro with "profound dehydration, nausea and vomiting." He first showed symptoms on January 1, but he continued to work his Kroger grocery management job even as his symptoms worsened. In the hospital, his condition deteriorated with "multiple systems failure," including "excessive nausea and vomiting, loose stools, skin rash, edema, dehydration, bone marrow damage, blood cell abnormalities, electrolyte abnormality, tachypnea (progressive shortness of breath), respiratory failure, tachycardia (fast heartbeat), low blood pressure, kidney malfunction and shutdown, and numbness and tingling in his hands and feet." The North Carolina Supreme Court later succinctly summed up this horrifying list: "Each of these symptoms is characteristic of arsenic poisoning," but no one suspected poisoning at the time.

Though Reid improved over several months of hospitalization and the doctors spoke of releasing him in early June, his condition took another plunge, and he was transferred to North Carolina Baptist Hospital in Winston-Salem on June 13. The list of dire symptoms lengthened, leading to partial paralysis. At the end of June, a lab report revealed "quite elevated" levels of arsenic, but his treating physician never saw that report and continued to treat what appeared to be Guillain-Barré.

After July, Reid once again began to improve. His attentive girlfriend got the doctor's permission to bring food for him from home. An intensive care unit (ICU) nurse wrote in her notes that Reid appeared well on October 1. Blanche was sitting by his bedside, feeding him some of her homemade banana pudding. Several witnesses said she brought him other treats: iced tea, McDonald's milkshakes, red Jell-O, soup and the Southern delicacy of corn bread soaked in milk.

On October 7, 1986, his body gave up the fight. Blanche said she didn't want an autopsy. "He has been through too much. He wouldn't want to be cut on like this. We just—we cannot have one."

Learning about Reid's 1986 death and Reverend Moore's illness—even without knowing all the details that connected them—was enough to prompt Dr. John Butts, the state's chief medical examiner, to ask the district attorney for an order to exhume Reid's body on June 13, 1989. The examination found "lethal concentrations of arsenic" and a medical history consistent with doses administered over a period of weeks.

Arsenic leaves an indelible mark on the body. Using the growth characteristics of hair, lab scientists can measure when and how much arsenic was introduced into a person. Over several months, Raymond Reid

Entrance to Wake Forest Baptist Hospital complex. *Courtesy of Anthony Crider via Wikimedia Commons.*

had periodically ingested varying amounts of arsenic. In a second-opinion review of the state lab's tests, Dr. Vincent Guinn, chemistry professor at the University of California–Irvine, also found evidence of multiple exposures to arsenic over a long period. By analyzing segments of hair, he found that the arsenic level was highest on June 24, measuring "roughly 70 times the normal level."

In an interview with journalist Russ Bowen, Dr. Butts described arsenic poisoning as a painful death. "People will become very ill, vomit, develop diarrhea, they may develop a rash, and then maybe a week or two later they'll develop neurological signs, these involve tingling, odd sensations, burning sensations, beginning in the hands and feet and then beginning to go centrally."

After finding the significant levels of arsenic in Raymond Reid's autopsy, Dr. Butts said, "They began a process of sort of examining all the folks who, as they used to joke about it, were deceased and had something to do with Blanche." They found witnesses at Kroger and other acquaintances who testified that she'd bought Anti-Ant poison—or asked someone to buy it for her. The active ingredient in Anti-Ant was arsenic.

Four more exhumations followed: Blanche's first husband, James Taylor, who died in 1973; her father, P.D. Kiser Sr.; her mother-in-law, Isla Taylor; and a co-worker, Joseph Mitchell. Lab tests showed Mitchell was the only one who left this world without aid from arsenic. Blanche's father and members of the Taylor family weren't so lucky. Her father's body showed high though not typically fatal levels of arsenic, but he wasn't physically strong and therefore could have been more susceptible at lower doses.

Blanche—a preacher's daughter, a preacher's wife, a grandmother, a ministering angel—was now accused of at least four poisoning murders.

Poison cases can be difficult to prosecute. Rarely does anyone witness the crime. And when the accused is a wife, a mother, a church lady, juries are often reluctant to convict. As this case unfolded in the press and eventually in court, many of those stereotypes of a typical Southern lady evaporated. Some who knew her described Blanche to investigators as duplicitous and vengeful when crossed. Blanche's upbringing was not genteel. Her father worked as a loom fixer in a local textile mill but was also an ordained Baptist minister and an abusive father with a gambling problem. At one point, he prostituted Blanche to pay his gambling debts. He died of a suspected heart attack in 1966, when Blanche was in her early thirties.

She had married James Napoleon Taylor in 1952, when she was nineteen, and they had two daughters. Taylor died in 1973 at age forty-five, also of a suspected heart attack. Forty-year-old Blanche had been flirting with Raymond Reid, one of the Kroger managers in Burlington, before they started dating.

As with any murder case, jurors and court-watchers wanted to know why, what motivated her to kill? Blanche took the stand at her trial but didn't admit or explain anything. As she had since her arrest (and maintained over the decades), she denied that she'd poisoned anyone.

Considering her childhood, armchair analysts said she hated men because she hated the alcoholic father who'd abandoned her mother for a younger woman and, at the same time, hypocritically stood in the pulpit and preached. She may well have hated men, but she always moved quickly from one to another. In an interview, Dwight Moore had a different take on what motivated her. "I think her motive was her inability to actually express her dissatisfaction with folks," he said, "and it was easier for her to do this than to say no."

Her sister Vanessa Woods shared another perspective with journalist Doug Struck: "Behind the headlines is a person who is not capable of doing this." But Forsyth County's district attorney Warren Sparrow countered: "We don't have to get into why," he said. "When you start looking for a rational motive, you generally start overthinking. I just know that this guy died and the state medical examiner said he had a fatal level of arsenic in him."

Blanche collected money from more than one of the deaths, as well as from a man who managed not to get poisoned but who, nonetheless, provided her with a payout. Blanche worked as a cashier at Kroger grocery. She was slender, attractive, always nicely dressed and personable with customers. She worked her way up to head cashier—a responsible position. After the widowed Blanche started dating co-worker Raymond Reid, she complained about R.H. (initials for privacy), one of Kroger's area managers. He propositioned her in an employee meeting room, and she ran out carrying his pants. In the sexual harassment lawsuit she filed a few months later, she claimed that the manager had a reputation for fondling female employees, that he'd made a crude advance to her at the store that day in October 1985 and that she couldn't return to work because the experience was so debilitating. Her lawsuit also alleged that she felt "completely alienated and antagonistic toward men and has not been able to maintain any meaningful social contacts with members of the opposite sex."

The 1980s saw an expanding cultural conversation about workplace sexual harassment, highlighted by the humorous hit movie *Nine to Five*, starring Jane Fonda, Lily Tomlin and Dolly Parton. As with many harassment cases, the allegations in Blanche's suit were never tested in court because Kroger paid her a reported $275,000 to settle the suit before trial.

That was a nice little nest egg, worth more than $700,000 today, but the lawsuit also delayed her courtship prospects. She'd been dating Raymond Reid, but not long before she quit working at Kroger, she met the Reverend Dwight Moore at an Easter sunrise service at the Carolina United Church of Christ. The preacher began escorting her to church events and calling on her. Questions arose later whether she was dating both men at the same time, trying to decide who would be the better prospect.

That question was answered in May 1986, when Raymond went to the hospital with nausea and with neuropathy in his hands and feet. Doctors diagnosed Guillain-Barré syndrome and its typical nerve numbness and prickling. Believed to be an autoimmune disorder that may be triggered by an infection, Guillain-Barré usually resolves itself within a month. For some patients, the pain and numbness linger.

Raymond Reid died five months later, in October 1986.

Because of her lawsuit—the one that claimed she'd been rendered "completely alienated and antagonistic toward men"—she told Dwight Moore she couldn't risk a public relationship with him. So the couple had to keep things quiet until the settlement was paid in July 1987.

In 1988, Blanche and Dwight Moore were planning a church wedding between Thanksgiving and the rush of Christmas Advent activities. They were forced to delay their plans when he was hospitalized for intestinal pain and two surgeries within two months.

Finally, on April 19, 1989, the couple was wed. Five days later, Dwight was in the hospital again with severe vomiting and diarrhea. Almost a month later, on May 13, doctors in the intensive care unit in Chapel Hill identified arsenic poisoning as the culprit.

After doctors called the SBI and its detectives interviewed Dwight, they spent several weeks investigating. During that time, Blanche continued to visit her husband in the hospital, just as she'd dutifully visited Raymond Reid. As Dwight lay in bed, still struggling with nerve pain and paralysis in his arms and legs and watching the telltale horizontal white Mees' lines—evidence of heavy metals poisoning, renal failure or chemotherapy treatment—as they grew outward from the cuticles of his fingernails, even faithful Dwight had to admit that the evidence against her convinced him. He told Blanche he didn't want to her to visit him anymore; he couldn't trust her.

Blanche was at her daughter's house when police came to arrest her on July 18, 1989. She was charged with Raymond Reid's first-degree murder

This building served as the Forsyth County Courthouse until a new building opened in 2023. *Courtesy of North Carolina Judicial Branch.*

but not charged with any of the other deaths. On October 15, 1990, her jury selection started in Winston-Salem, in Forsyth County, where Raymond had died, and not in Alamance County, where Blanche lived. Blanche took the stand to defend herself—a risky move for any defendant. She said she saw Raymond fed only through a tube at the hospital. He didn't eat any food, and she'd certainly not brought him banana pudding or peanut butter milkshakes. She didn't remember any conversations about an autopsy, and she wouldn't have opposed one. Plenty of other witnesses had already testified in the state's case, and the jury would decide where the truth lay.

One month after the trial started, the jury found her guilty of first-degree murder. During the penalty phase, jurors can weigh aggravating and mitigating circumstances in considering the appropriateness of the death penalty. This jury found two aggravating circumstances that made her death-penalty eligible under North Carolina law: that she killed for pecuniary gain and that Raymond's long illness and death from arsenic poisoning was "especially heinous, atrocious or cruel." The jury also found mitigating circumstances: that she "provided well for her children as they were growing up," that she submitted peacefully to arrest and that she showed "concern and kindness for others in her community." The jury recommended the death penalty.

She appealed her conviction, arguing in part that the jury shouldn't have heard about the death of James Taylor and the poisoning of Dwight Moore. The appellate court answered her objection:

> *Three different men either married to or intimately involved with defendant died, or barely escaped death, from arsenic poisoning, an unusual cause of death. In each case defendant had motive (financial), opportunity (close relationship), and means (knowledge of and access to Anti-Ant). In each case medical evidence suggests that multiple doses of arsenic were administered to the victim over a long period of time, as opposed to one large fatal dose. In each case defendant was frequently alone with the victim in the hospital, and medical testimony suggests that certain of defendant's visits in which she fed the victim corresponded with an onset of symptoms characteristic of arsenic poisoning. In each case defendant was heard to say that she hated the victim or that the victim was cruel or evil. In the cases of Reid and Taylor, defendant was already seeing her next victim at the time of the arsenic assaults.*

The court upheld her conviction and death sentence.

Blanche was tried only for Raymond Reid's murder. In a case of multiple murders, district attorneys must calculate which case will be strongest in front of a jury, which has the most persuasive and damning evidence. But as journalist Taft Wireback noted, the ghost of one of North Carolina's other famous female serial poisoners hovered over Blanche's trial. Velma Barfield was tried in eastern North Carolina in 1978. Joe Freeman Britt, one of the deadliest prosecutors in the United States, presented evidence of Velma's earlier victims when he won a death-penalty verdict. He'd tried thirteen death-penalty cases and won convictions in each one, all in a period of seventeen months. In the 1980s, *People* magazine said Britt was single-handedly responsible for 4 percent of the nation's death penalty verdicts. Velma's attorneys unsuccessfully appealed her conviction, claiming that bringing in other deaths in order to show a pattern of criminal conduct or homicidal behavior was improper, especially where the evidence wasn't strong enough for the prosecutors to feel comfortable bringing those other cases to trial. In Velma's case, the state appellate court disagreed with the defense, which left the door open for Blanche's prosecutors to mention the other bodies exhumed and the arsenic levels found in James Taylor and Dwight Moore.

High-profile trials can have their odd or unexpected moments. For one, criminal cases are rarely intermingled with civil cases—but Blanche's case was connected with two civil cases: her sexual harassment lawsuit and a medical malpractice case brought by Raymond Reid's family. The lawsuit over his medical care happened to provide evidence that bolstered her prosecution.

Also rare are confessions from beyond the grave. A jailer testified in Blanche's trial that a local man, Garvin Thomas, had tried to visit her while she was held in the Alamance County Jail. He came bearing a teddy bear. The jailer said Garvin claimed that "he had done so much wrong in his life and hurt so many people that he wanted to start doing some good to right the wrongs." A few months later, just before he died, he wrote a letter confessing to the three poisonings linked to Blanche. He wrote to "My Dearest Darling" and admitted that he'd long admired her and was jealous of the other men in her life.

The prosecution's handwriting expert said Blanche had written the confession letter. W.A. Shulenberger, the defense expert, had an illustrious career with the SBI and the U.S. Treasury Department. He'd examined questioned documents tracing Lee Harvey Oswald's movements before the Kennedy assassination, fraudster Billie Sol Estes $17 million swindle and signatures in the fraud trial involving Jim and Tammy Bakker's PTL Club downfall in Charlotte. Shulenberger testified that Blanche could not have written the letter, though he couldn't confirm that Garvin had written it. While the teddy bear and the deathbed confession letter provided diversions, they didn't change the course of the trial.

Reverend Dwight Moore survived a poisoned chicken salad sandwich he ate five days after their wedding as well as Blanche's treat-bearing visits to his hospital bed. But he continued to have as reminders of that period in his life the constant pain and neuropathy left behind by arsenic levels higher than any of his doctors had ever seen, at one point over one hundred times the normal amount.

Part of Blanche's legend was her reputation as a gentle caregiver who visited her husband and her boyfriend in the hospital, bringing their favorite foods to help nourish them. The truth, though, was chilling; the church lady on her visits of mercy was actually spooning arsenic-laced banana pudding into each victim as he lay in intensive care. Evidence shows that Raymond Reid received his final fatal arsenic dose in his hospital bed, his body wracked with nerve pain and his skin swollen and cracked.

A book and numerous articles were written about the case, and Elizabeth Montgomery of *Bewitched* fame starred in a TV movie (*Black Widow Murders*), bringing even more notoriety to the case.

Blanche was sentenced in 1990 for Raymond Reid's death. Less than three weeks later, husband Dwight Moore formally filed for divorce. In 2024, she continued to hold the honor of being the oldest woman on death row in the United States.

ROBERT COULTHARD AND THE PERFECT FAMILY

In December 1986, just months after she delivered her second baby, thirty-year-old Sandy Coulthard began suffering recurring bouts of illness. She and her husband, Robert, were also parents of a young toddler, and the family lived in High Point, at the heart of North Carolina's booming furniture industry. The Coulthards met and began dating when they were students at Wake Forest University, and thirty-year-old Robert, a sales executive, had continued his wife's family tradition in the region's furniture industry.

The couple were active members at Emerywood Baptist Church. When their first child arrived, Sandy gave up her job teaching special-needs children in Randolph County schools. To those who knew them, they

Wait Chapel was the first building constructed on Wake Forest College's Reynolda campus in 1956 and remains a centerpiece of the university. *Courtesy of almassengale via Flickr.*

were the portrait of a happy, successful family—the perfect couple, said their friends.

Sandy's first attack of nausea and vomiting appeared to be a viral illness. Fortunately, Robert had just returned home from a business trip and could help her with the children. In the first of her three visits in January 1988, her doctor suspected chicken pox.

The attacks continued at intervals, and in June, Sandy was admitted to High Point Regional Hospital, then transferred to Duke University Medical Center, where she remained for eleven more days. At Duke, her condition improved. The nausea, vomiting and numbness in her extremities led doctors to suspect Guillain-Barré syndrome, a rare immune system attack on the body's nervous system. On or before July 3, she became alert enough to accept an ice chip or sip of soft drink her husband offered her. Soon after, her symptoms returned with a vengeance.

After suffering for almost seven months, she died on July 9. Her body had bloated so severely her skin was cracking, but a battery of tests during her hospital stays hadn't revealed what caused her illness and death.

However, tests from her initial autopsy revealed higher than normal amounts of arsenic. As a result, her body was exhumed for a more complete forensic autopsy and drug screen. The medical investigators needed to learn more about her condition before they could confirm what had caused the young mother to die.

One of the detectives called in to investigate was reminded of a *Reader's Digest* article on the death of Napoleon and how strands of his hair revealed systematic exposure to arsenic leading up to his death. Could that technique chart the progression in this case? Arsenic is a heavy metal that settles into hair, fingernails and bone. Human hair, on average, grows one centimeter or roughly one-third of an inch per month, and strands can detail with remarkable clarity the timing of prolonged doses of arsenic. Tests on Napoleon were possible because his head was shaved after his death in order to leave locks for family and friends—a tradition at the time. Decades later, those hair samples revealed long-term exposure and high concentrations in Napoleon's body, leading to speculation that he was murdered. Was he fed arsenic? Or was he exposed to high levels from gas-emitting arsenic-dyed wallpaper or fabrics in places where he was held in exile? He also had stomach cancer (which had killed his father) and had been treated with mercurous chloride (a strong, potentially damaging and poisonous emetic) shortly before he died. One set of researchers believed his medical treatment killed him, holding that he died *with* arsenic poisoning—whether homicidal or accidental—but not *of* it. His locks of hair remain the classic demonstration of arsenic as a measuring stick for murder.

Hair samples recovered at Sandy Coulthard's autopsy mapped her slow murder, starting just months after her second child was born.

According to those tests, Sandy received her first dose of arsenic in late December 1987 or early January, followed by a nonfatal dose in February or March. In June, after her husband returned from yet another business trip—one he'd taken with another woman—he apparently put his plan into high gear with the help of fast-food hamburgers he brought home as a dinner treat. To Sandy, her burger tasted odd, and she didn't eat much of it. She soon started vomiting, which prompted the trip to High Point Regional Hospital and later transfer to Duke. If she'd eaten more of the hamburger, the dose might have been fatal.

Though she began to improve in the hospital, she apparently received another dose on July 3, either in ice or in a drink—this time sufficient to kill her, eleven days after she'd been moved to Duke.

In eliminating other possible sources of exposure, investigators narrowed down individuals who could have given her the earlier doses and the final fatal dose: her parents, her brother or her husband. Linking their visits to her bouts of illness, all but one of those people could be eliminated: her husband, Robert Coulthard. According to Guilford County district attorney Jim Kimel, doctors' and nurses' notes in her medical records indicated that Robert was "the only one who had access to her during the time the dose would have been administered."

When the nine-week investigation was finalized, Robert F. Coulthard Jr. was charged with first-degree murder in September 1988. He pleaded guilty weeks later but never explained his motive.

That left investigators, family and friends to speculate. According to *Charlotte Observer* crime reporter Elizabeth Leland, he had become fond of the lifestyle he enjoyed after he married into Sandy Coles's family. He also grew fond of gambling, racking up about $25,000 in debt, and he enjoyed squiring around other women. His phone records told investigators he'd called one of those women from the Duke Medical Center while Sandy was fighting to live. Assistant District Attorney Richard Lyle argued that a divorce would've meant giving up things he valued, like his job, the money he'd owe for alimony and his standing with the Coles family and in the community.

Davidson College professor Cynthia Lewis cited the Coulthard case, along with Michael Peterson and Rae Carruth—other North Carolina wife killers (see *Triangle True Crime Stories* and *Charlotte True Crime Stories* for more on those cases)—in examining why husbands or boyfriends kill. Women are far more likely to be killed by an intimate partner, according to U.S. Department of Justice statistics—30 percent of murdered women versus only 3 or 4 percent of men are killed by their partners. A pregnant woman is more than twice as likely to become a victim of her partner. That was an unusual factor in the Coulthard case—he waited until she wasn't pregnant. As Detective Mark McNeill, who worked the case, explained to Professor Lewis, Robert didn't *not* love his wife or his children. But he loved his lavish lifestyle and his freedom more. In Professor Lewis's interview with Detective McNeill, he said, "This wasn't an emotional crime. It wasn't a crime of passion. It wasn't the usual spouse-killing. It was a practical matter." And his lack of emotion, his careful calculation and his attempts to maintain the façade of the ideal family "didn't leave traces of emotion for even his wife to pick up on." Robert was able to hide his self-centeredness in plain sight.

In a tragic turn in the case, investigators learned that medical tests showed the presence of arsenic in Sandy's body nine days before her death—but that didn't save her. On June 26, when she was hospitalized after eating part of a hamburger, a doctor ordered a toxic heavy metals blood profile. Days before she received the fatal dose and before she died on July 9, 1988, the tests showed dangerously high levels of arsenic in her blood, but the results weren't requested by physicians, forwarded or acted on.

That oversight prompted her parents to file, on behalf of Sandy's children, a medical malpractice case against Duke University Medical Center, High Point Regional Hospital and six physicians and their medical practices.

Identifying arsenic as the source of her illness days before her death couldn't guarantee the medical team would have had time to save Sandy's life. In another North Carolina poisoning case involving the Raleigh death of Dr. Eric Miller, a medical records error prevented physicians from learning about high arsenic levels in his blood for ten days. The young father died the day after treatment began. Even with quick intervention, poisoning victims don't always survive, but common sense says a proper diagnosis might have improved Sandy's odds. It could also have prevented Robert from feeding his wife the final, fatal dose just as she was showing signs of improvement.

John Trestrail, author of *Criminal Poisoning: An Investigational Guide*, used FBI crime statistics to show how rare poisoning deaths are: in 1999, only 11 homicides of the 12,658 reported that year resulted from poison.

Trestrail's research showed that, among those rare poisoning deaths, the clear majority—about 30 percent—were caused by arsenic. The second most popular choice among poisoners was cyanide, which accounted for only 9 percent of poisoning homicides. Though poisoning deaths are dramatically eclipsed by gun or beating deaths, arsenic isn't an antiquated relic left over from Agatha Christie novels. It remains remarkably easy to slip poison past medical detection because it mimics normal diseases, even with modern lab testing. It's so rare and unexpected, it becomes almost invisible.

Once investigators knew what to look for in Sandy's case, they methodically pieced together a timeline of Robert's activities. In September 1986, soon after he got home from a business trip where he "established a relationship" with a woman, he ordered a packet of arsenic from a New Jersey chemical lab—enough to kill 2,500 people, reported journalist Elizabeth Leland—and paid $160 with his personal check. That check was one of the first clear links for investigators. Robert patiently waited until four months after their son was born, after Sandy had finished breastfeeding, before he put his long-incubated plan into action. According to the SBI, when she died, Sandy's body contained 142 times the normal amount of arsenic found in a human body.

Robert had also purchased $351,000 in life insurance on Sandy months before she showed the first signs of arsenic poisoning—more than twice what they'd paid for their home in a popular High Point neighborhood.

Once Robert was arrested, the battleground shifted from the hospitals and doctors to the courthouse and its lawyers and judge. The charge would be first-degree murder. Would it be a death penalty case? Or would Robert Coulthard face life in prison? In North Carolina, as in other states with the death penalty, a homicide must demonstrate one or more aggravating circumstances before the defendant faces death. Aggravating circumstances include killing for pecuniary gain or a crime that is especially heinous, atrocious or cruel—crueler than an "ordinary" homicide. A defendant with no significant history of prior criminal activity could have a mitigating circumstance and perhaps avoid the death penalty.

In a November 1988 court hearing, the district attorney stated that Sandy's death did not involve any of the aggravating circumstances required by state law. The children were the beneficiaries of the insurance policies, not Robert. And the prosecutor didn't challenge the assessment given by her doctors that she'd been in no pain. As a result, the judge ruled that Coulthard's conduct was not bad enough to merit a possible death sentence. The worse that Robert Coulthard faced was life in prison with the possibility of parole.

Robert surprised court watchers. He paused only seconds after the judge asked the routine question about his plea before he answered "guilty." Prior to the hearing, Robert's defense attorneys had outlined for him the evidence against him. With the death penalty off the table, he agreed to admit that he'd killed his wife. He didn't, however, explain why. District attorney Kimel said, "He stood up, the judge gave him life and that was it."

The judge's decision that he wasn't eligible to face the death penalty generated a point of debate for this case and for future cases. In most states, murder by poison is a death-penalty offense.

The key question here: Was arsenic poisoning a painful way to die? In Blanche Taylor Moore's case, the district attorney successfully argued that arsenic poisoning meant a cruel, painful death. In Robert Coulthard's case, though, prosecutors asked the physicians who treated Sandy at Duke Medical whether she suffered. "We specifically asked the attending doctors, 'How much pain was she in?'" District Attorney Kimel told the *Greensboro News & Record*. Her doctors said she "wasn't in any pain." That assessment meant Robert Coulthard didn't face the death penalty.

But did the doctors give an unbiased assessment? Most experts would argue that death by poison is "especially cruel." In South Carolina, poison is specifically listed as a death penalty–eligible aggravating circumstance—no room left for argument. Perhaps the doctors were saying they'd successfully managed her pain. Or perhaps they had their eye on the medical malpractice suits filed by Sandy's family.

When Robert was sentenced, "life" in North Carolina allowed for parole reviews. In 1994, the state instituted a sentence of "life without parole," but Robert's sentence provided for a first review after twenty years. At his first parole hearing in 2008, Sandy's family and friends presented two thousand signatures on petitions and hundreds of letters asking that his parole be denied. Petitioners included the detectives who'd investigated her death. Guilford County district attorney Douglas Henderson said, "This is one of the most coldly calculated, deliberate and premeditated killings that we have ever seen in our jurisdiction." Robert was denied parole but remains eligible for reconsideration in following years. The process is difficult for both families. Robert's family continues to support him. His cousin Jim Coulthard said he'd never seen signs of violence or psychopathy, only a young man whose "period of indiscretion" led him away from the values his parents instilled in him.

As of this writing, Robert Coulthard remained incarcerated in North Carolina. While he's accumulated remarkably few infractions (nine in the years since 1988 when he entered the system), he stepped up the pace and severity in 2017—the last year he was cited—logging three offenses in one year, one for weapon possession.

2

UNSOLVED

THE COFFEE POT CASE

On August 24, 1892, a Winston-Salem newspaper reported an unusual case of a poisoned coffee pot.

Mrs. William Sides (as the newspaper identified her) and her two children—a twenty-two-year-old son and a daughter "about eighteen"—attended a country church on Sunday, August 21, near Clemmonsville (now called Clemmons), a township southwest of Winston-Salem. Church services and perhaps some visiting kept them "the greater part of the day away from home."

The next morning, after they ate breakfast, the three became ill with violent vomiting. Dr. Griffith made a house call, and once he saw how seriously ill they were, he called Dr. Summers for help. They identified the illness as poisoning and linked it to white powder they found in the family's coffee pot.

Apparently, Monday morning's coffee had been made with fresh grounds added to those left over from Sunday. On Sunday, the pot sat in the kitchen while the family was away at church, and as was their custom, they'd left the kitchen door unlocked. The physicians took "about a teaspoonful of the white powder" to test and identified it as "a very large quantity of arsenic."

Clemmons Village Hall sign. *Courtesy of Smallfry918 via Wikimedia Commons.*

When the newspapers went to press on Tuesday, the son was "about out of danger." Mrs. Sides and her daughter were in critical condition, but by Wednesday, they were expected to recover. One of the oddities of arsenic poisoning is that too much all at once just might save your life. Arsenic causes vomiting, and a large amount may irritate the stomach enough to purge much of the poison. That natural process may well have saved the lives of Mrs. Sides and her children. That they were all relatively young and healthy didn't hurt.

No one seemed to know who tried to kill the threesome. One newspaper could only blame it on "some scoundrel who entered the house." No mention was made of a Mr. Sides, and no follow-up to the case could be found in the local papers. Some small-town mysteries remain just that—unsolved and puzzling with the secret suspicions that neighbors likely shared only with one another.

THE PARTY PEOPLE

Would a male funeral home worker have noticed that the young woman's clothes weren't right? The female worker certainly did as soon as she saw the body on the mortuary slab. The stockings and underwear were turned inside out. "No woman ever dressed herself like that," said other funeral home workers who saw the body.

On January 13, 1929, the body of twenty-two-year-old Nellie Jones Ballinger was discovered by an eight-year-old neighbor girl. The girl's mother had sent her to "make a borrowing" at Nellie's mother's house at 1110 South Pearson Street in Greensboro. She came in through the unlocked door and found Nellie in the front room, the one to the left of the front door. She was lying on her side near the fireplace. Very little blood was visible, but a .32-caliber Smith & Wesson revolver belonging to Nellie's family lay beside her, only one bullet fired.

From when Nellie was last seen and from forensic evidence, investigators determined she'd likely died on Sunday, two days before she was discovered. Neighbors had seen a light burning in the front room since Sunday night, but no one heard a gunshot. Given the scene, the first assumption was that she'd died by suicide, though a search uncovered no note. She had recently made the then-novel move of filing for divorce. Before no-fault divorces were made law, a divorce filing required grounds; she claimed cruelty and desertion by her husband.

Questions quickly arose. Friends said Nellie simply wouldn't kill herself. Friends and family often respond that way to such a tragedy, but those who'd seen her immediately before her death and those who'd known her over time said it didn't make sense. She'd stayed at Greensboro's King Cotton Hotel for a few days, moved in temporarily with her mother and was looking for a boardinghouse room. She was having fun, planning her future.

Physical evidence soon made her death look like something very different from suicide. Why wasn't there a bullet hole in her dress? Did she shoot herself through her left breast and into her heart while she was naked, then proceed to dress herself in a jumble of clothing? Or, as an investigator later suggested, did she awkwardly jam a gun inside the neck of her dress and shoot herself? He seemed to be the only one who thought that was plausible.

The lack of blood where she lay and the reduced amount of blood remaining in her body when she was embalmed pointed to her being killed elsewhere and then moved to the front room in her mother's house. But where was she killed? And why? And, most importantly, by whom?

King Cotton Hotel, Greensboro, N. C.

111792

A 1928 postcard for King Cotton Hotel in Greensboro, where Nellie Ballinger stayed in the days before she was killed. *Card by Willis Book & Stationery, Curt Teich, from author's collection.*

Her husband, Ernest Ballinger, was safely out of contention as a suspect—at the time of Nellie's death, he was in Panama serving as a naval officer on the USS *Texas*.

On the evening of January 17, 1929, the coroner's inquest heard the evidence of the women at the funeral home about her inside-out clothing. They also testified that she had bruises on her neck and shoulder and had no bullet hole in her dress—reported as "a factor which was largely responsible for the verdict of murder," even though the lead investigator, Captain L.B. Wrenn, believed it was a case of suicide. He even demonstrated how she could have put the muzzle of the pistol down the neck of her dress with her left hand. The jury, according to press reports, noted that she clutched a clean handkerchief in her left hand. How could she have held the gun as described in the captain's awkward reenactment? After much deliberation, the jury unanimously and on their first ballot found her death to be homicide at the hands of a person or persons unknown. "Nothing was divulged during the inquest that would throw any light on the guilt of any particular party or indicate the motive for the death of the woman," said the news report.

With her husband's frequent absences during their two-year marriage, Nellie had developed a reputation as a party girl. The coroner's jury heard about three cars parked in front of her mother's house on that Sunday and a "wild party" that officials planned to investigate. News reports later said Nellie had been riding in a red roadster late Sunday afternoon with four cadets wearing Oak Ridge Military Academy uniforms. A neighbor overheard a young businessman exchanging harsh words with Nellie at her mother's house on Sunday evening, but police withheld his name. He told police he hadn't seen Nellie for two weeks but admitted they'd kept company. Letters he'd written to her were found in the front room scattered around her body.

She'd also been associated with Robert George Smith, a sixty-four-year-old bachelor with his own reputation about town—and his own mysterious murder. The retired clothing salesman lived in the country off Randleman Road near the border between Guilford and Randolph Counties. The newspaper ran a photo of him stooped over playing with two little lambs, the essence of a gentleman farmer. But rumors in Greensboro spoke of wild sex orgies that drew guests from around the area to his rambling farmhouse.

On September 5, 1929, a friend stopped by Robert's house to see if he wanted to go squirrel hunting. He found him dead inside his house, killed by a blast from a 16-gauge shotgun to the back of his head. His assailant had apparently fired from outside through the open downstairs window. His death occurred almost eight months after Nellie's, but because of the party rumors and the oddity of the two deaths, they became linked.

As often happens when a case lingers unsolved, the speculation wandered far afield. Friends said Robert Smith wore a diamond stickpin that was now missing and should be traced; his brother said he knew Robert often invested in jewelry, but he'd never seen a diamond stickpin. Someone else said that "just before" he was shot, Robert had been out on the road with a shovel repairing a pothole. Others said he wouldn't have been wearing a diamond stickpin to do road repair, so it was unlikely it was stolen from his body after the shooting. All this debate was carefully covered by the newspapers.

A month after Robert's death, his brother came from Charlotte to begin probate on the estate and announced he would add $1,000 to the state and county reward for information. According to a news report, investigations by the sheriff and the coroner's jury "netted nothing but clues" and no clear answers The increased award (worth about $17,000 today) also failed to net anything that led to a suspect.

Armchair detectives are not a new phenomenon. On March 4, 1929, a reader, J.W.B., wrote to the *Greensboro Record*: "I've kept quiet long enough. I've listened to murder theories and to suicide until I've got a big enough collection on hand to write a first class detective story about….Why isn't some one arrested?…I believe the principal witnesses involved in the tangle know a little more about the thing than they let on." J.W.B. didn't share his key suspect, unfortunately. The murders of Nellie Ballinger and Robert Smith remain unsolved.

THE TRAGIC MEETING OF WEALTH AND FAME

The Triad region is home to some of the South's largest and most influential companies. The era of the robber barons and their corporate trusts created the kinds of fortunes still on display at Asheville's Biltmore House, built by railroad baron Cornelius Vanderbilt. While James B. Duke's tobacco trust wasn't as large as the oil or railroad trusts of the period, its influence was still significant—and continued to be important to North Carolina. Duke's name is on the $11 billion Duke Endowment,

Duke University, Duke Energy and the Duke Mansion in Charlotte. A 1911 federal anti-monopoly case led to the court-ordered dissolution of Duke's American Tobacco Company into four resulting companies (American Tobacco, R.J. Reynolds, Liggett & Myers and Lorillard), which continued to wield significant financial power in the state. In particular, the money held by corporate owners in the Duke family and the Reynolds family left its mark in their magnificent homes, their charitable bequests and the family scandals that seem invariably to find their way into the lives of the wealthy. Fortunes can't insulate families from tragedy and sadness.

R.J. Reynolds, founder of R.J. Reynolds Tobacco Company, built Reynolda House in Winston-Salem for his young family. R.J. died in 1918, leaving his wife—thirty years his junior—and four children. When his widow died six years later, the youngest child, Z. Smith Reynolds, was only six years old. The children were raised by an aunt and uncle.

As a teenager, Smith was known as an energetic risk-taker with little time for formal schooling. Swept up in the excitement of Charles Lindbergh's 1927 transatlantic flight, he became one of the country's youngest licensed pilots. He made what looked like a propitious, if very young, marriage to the heir of North Carolina's Cannon Mills textiles fortune, but they had a child and were divorced in short order.

Terrace and pool at Reynolda House in 1919, photographed by Thomas Warren Sears. *Courtesy of Wikimedia Commons.*

Nineteen-year-old Smith Reynolds became fascinated with "torch singer" and actress Libby Holman, more than seven years his senior. Six days after his divorce, the couple eloped and married quietly in November 1931. Almost immediately, Smith left on an around-the-world flight, first traveling to Hong Kong via Cairo, Baghdad and Hanoi. His plane stranded him in China, and Libby joined him in April 1932, five months after they wed, for a honeymoon.

She had already had an active and increasingly successful career in New York, a better singer than she was an actress. She enjoyed the parties, meeting people, the excitement. At first, she hadn't taken Smith's infatuation seriously, but he apparently grew on her.

On July 5, 1932, Libby and Smith held one of their famous weekend parties at Reynolda, complete with bootleg liquor flowing despite Prohibition. After the party wound down and most of the guests headed home, reports about what happened in the early morning hours were fuzzy. Not unusual, given the amount of alcohol consumed and the late hour. Libby, Smith and Smith's longtime friend Albert "Ab" Walker were staying at the house. Just past midnight, Smith was on the sleeping porch next to the master bedroom cleaning his .32-caliber automatic pistol. In a jealous scene common for the couple, he had been accusing Libby of flirting with his friends at the party, especially Ab, who was downstairs

Z. Smith Reynolds in 1931, at age nineteen. *Photo courtesy of Wikimedia Commons.*

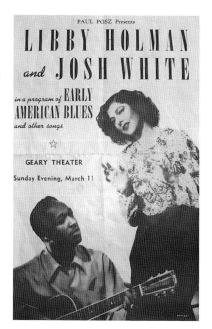

Music program featuring Libby Holman and Josh White appearing at Geary Theater. *Photo courtesy of bunky's pickle via Flickr.*

when he heard a single shot. Libby said she was asleep when Smith stumbled in from the porch and fell on the bed.

Was something untoward happening between Ab and Libby? Was Smith distraught over that? Had the depression that had prompted him to threaten suicide on other occasions swept over him again? Or had something more sinister happened?

Smith suffered a single gunshot wound to his right temple, but he was still alive. Libby and Ab didn't wait for the ambulance; they carried him to the car and rushed him to Winston-Salem's Baptist Hospital. He died within hours.

Given his energetic, mercurial personality, suicide seemed a logical explanation. But in August, a coroner's jury listened to evidence, including Libby's unclear memories of a gun and Smith falling and testimony from their friends, and indicted Libby for first-degree murder and Ab as an accessory.

Libby's attorneys negotiated her surrender to the sheriff in Rockingham County, about forty miles from Reynolda. Officials calculated it would be less likely to attract the New York tabloid press, which was feasting on the story. Before the hearing, she checked into the Belvedere Hotel in nearby Reidsville and was driven the few miles to the courthouse in Wentworth. The choice of quiet Wentworth hadn't kept everyone away. A crowd of maybe five hundred waited for her on the courthouse grounds. Word had gotten out. Locals were selling food and drink from wagons. Photographers and reporters swarmed, one catching a poignant photo of her inside the courtroom wearing her widow's veil, awaiting the proceedings.

Belvedere Hotel in Reidsville, North Carolina. *Courtesy of Durwood Barbour Collection of North Carolina Postcards, UNC Libraries Commons.*

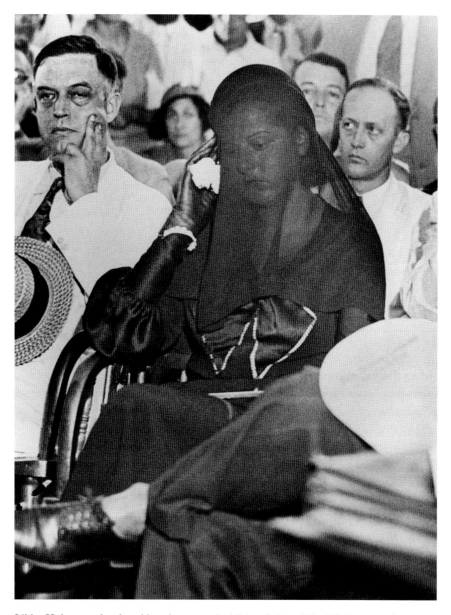

Libby Holman at her bond hearing, seated with her father, Alfred Holman, and Reidsville physician Dr. M.P. Cummings. *Photo by unnamed press photographer, courtesy of Wikimedia Commons.*

At the hearing, charges were reduced, and the two posted $25,000 in bail. Later, the charges were dropped. Eventually, the story came out that the couple's friends had been less than honest at the inquest. *No, they hadn't drunk to excess*, they said. *The party was quiet and orderly.* Some felt the initial charges were brought against Libby and Ab to force the witnesses to be truthful about what happened. Events remained cloudy.

Libby was pregnant, which affected loyalties for the Reynolds family. Though Smith had enjoyed the freedom and luxury of a wealthy young man, he wouldn't come into his own inheritance until age twenty-eight. A baby complicated the family's reaction to Smith's death.

Smith's older brother Dick was adventuring the world on his freighter and was docked in the Canary Islands when he got word of his brother's death. He refused to believe the suicide theory, and when he returned home, he had his brother's body secretly exhumed. The autopsy, conducted by four surgeons, added more controversy to the case. According to Heidi Schnakenberg's biography of Dick Reynolds, "The result of the autopsy suggested [Smith] was shot at close range—a distance of three to five feet—rather than point-blank—a distance of less than three feet and much more common during a suicide, as the original coroner's report stated."

With that much money, that much fame and that much opportunity for embarrassment, few were surprised when the family didn't object to the dismissal of the charges. In fact, as summarized in *Vanity Fair*, Smith's uncle Will, an executive with Reynolds Tobacco Company, had written the state solicitor, saying Smith's family would not "'find any pleasure in a prosecution not fully justified by the circumstances of his death.'"

Was quietly dismissing the case the influence of the family's status and wealth or simply a practical kindness for a grieving family? Given the evidence available, getting a conviction would have been difficult. Testing at the time indicated that the gun had not been close enough to Smith's head to cause stippling, which weighed against suicide. But how accurate were those tests? His history of suicide threats was hard to ignore. And the family wasn't pushing for a criminal trial. After all, the baby's mother could block their access to Smith's child, if she chose to. Such family matters required diplomacy.

Baby Christopher Reynolds was born on January 11, 1933, in Philadelphia. Inevitably, a battle over the estate raged. Had he lived, Smith would have inherited $20 million from his parents' estate when he turned twenty-eight (over $450 million today). The family settled $7 million on Libby and Christopher. Smith's brother Dick used his share of Smith's estate to open the Z. Smith Reynolds Foundation, which continues to invest in charitable projects around the state. Young Christopher, who was the image of Smith, died at age seventeen in a fall while climbing with a friend on California's Mount Whitney. Mountain climbing was his passion, just as flying had been his father's; he died shortly before he was to enroll as a freshman at Dartmouth College.

In 2023, discussing with a *Garden & Gun* writer the first ever exhibit on Smith Reynolds's death, Reynolda Museum curator Phil Archer said, "When you start comparing all the different stories, there's so much that doesn't add up....Whether there was a crime or not, there was certainly a cover-up." The tragic lives of millionaire heir Smith Reynolds and Broadway singer Libby Holman remain, at the end, shrouded in mystery.

3

THE LOVELORN

A NORTH CAROLINA CRIME FIRST

Given her upbringing in the late 1800s and her physical description, Ida Bell Warren sounded like an unremarkably ordinary North Carolina woman. Her father was a Confederate veteran left with daughter Ida to raise after his wife died. When he remarried, Ida and her new stepmother didn't get along—a story as common in life as in fairy tales. Ida ran away and later returned home with a baby daughter of her own, Pearl, but with no husband.

Ida was described in news accounts as large and squat with heavy or coarse features. But she must have had a certain charm about her, for her life was not devoid of lovers. In 1908, she met Samuel Christy in Winston-Salem and soon left for Texas with him and her daughter. Sam, described as "a little man with a slender white face and no chin to speak of," was already married and a father, but that didn't impede their plans.

The couple ran a boardinghouse in Grand Saline, Texas, about an hour east of Dallas. Garret Warren was one of their guests. Though he was thirteen years younger than Ida, Garret Warren was quite taken with her. The railroad man invited her to come away with him back to North Carolina, and she took him up on his offer. She stole $400 from Sam Christy—all his savings, reportedly—and she and Garret left for Winston-Salem, where they married.

Staying in Texas, Sam eventually married another woman and had two sons. However, in 1914, when Ida contacted him and invited him to come to Winston-Salem, he traveled to see her. She'd decided, for reasons never fully explained, that she wanted Garret Warren out of the way, permanently. She needed some help, and Sam was willing.

Sam stayed with Ida at the home of her daughter, Pearl, who'd married Clifford Stonestreet when she was about fifteen years old. At the kitchen table, Sam and Ida talked over how best to get rid of Ida's husband. Early in the morning of August 18, 1914, according to Ida's testimony, she administered chloroform to Garret, and Sam strangled him to death with help from Clifford. The rumor persisted that Clifford had done the strangling, but that wasn't the story Ida told.

They loaded the body in a trunk, lifted it onto a rented wagon, battered his face in an attempt to make it unrecognizable and dumped his body in Muddy Creek south of Winston-Salem. They buried the trunk and Garret's clothing in the basement at Pearl and Clifford Stonestreet's house. The body remained hidden until April, when it surfaced during a flood and some fishermen discovered it.

When Garret first went missing, the railroad he worked for had no reason to worry about him. Ida told them he'd gone to Louisiana to see family. But when his mother wrote the railroad, asking about her son, Ida had to answer more questions, this time from the police.

Even after Ida Bell Warren, Samuel Christy and Clifford Stonestreet—the accused perpetrators of the Muddy Creek Murder Mystery, as the newspapers called it—were tried and convicted, questions still wafted around the case. Most didn't think the defendants were accurately matched with their crimes. Clifford was sentenced as an accessory and Sam and Ida as murderers. Though most didn't think Sam had killed Garret Warren, they agreed he'd likely been the one to dump the body in Muddy Creek.

Ida Bell Warren became the first woman sentenced to die in North Carolina's electric chair. When their trial ended, the convicted killers bid farewell to their jailers, shaking

North Carolina's electric chair in Raleigh. *Courtesy of State Archives of North Carolina via Flickr.*

Greensboro's Southern Railway Station. *Courtesy of Warren LeMay via Flickr.*

hands and offering many thanks for their kind care before and during the trial. When the twosome boarded the train in Winston-Salem, headed for prison in Raleigh, they were dressed for travel—Sam clean-shaven and wearing a blue serge suit, Ida in the blue dress she wore to her trial. Reporters described both as being nervous, their hands trembling as they gave short interviews.

By the time the train made the short nighttime trip to Greensboro, the reporters tracking their journey said they seemed calm, not nervous. This train trip was the first time the two had seen each other since their trial, and they shared a meal from a tray placed between them on the bench at the Greensboro railway station, eating heartily despite the cumbersome handcuffs. To reporters, both repeated what they'd said all along: they were innocent, they hadn't killed Garret Warren. Both of course hoped their death sentences would be commuted by the governor.

Even as the couple traveled toward Raleigh and the Death House in Central Prison, women's groups around the country were working on Ida Bell Warren's behalf, circulating petitions and drawing press attention to her looming execution date. Justice moved quickly in those days.

North Carolina governor's mansion on Blount Street in Raleigh, first occupied in 1891. *Courtesy of Library of Congress Prints and Photographs Division.*

According to the *Lenoir News* report, some of the "agitation" against executing her came from an "ancient chivalry of mannerism" while others had a more "modern" view of saving a woman's life "whose sin is largely of man's making."

In March 1916, Governor Craig was wrestling with moral and practical arguments against any more executions. Twenty-five men had died in the state's electric chair in a seven-year span; five of those had died in the last thirty days. The prison warden, burdened with the constant pressure of the executions and an illness that had "shattered" his nerves, had himself died recently. If Ida and Sam were executed, Raleigh's death row would then be empty of inmates.

Some observers said the events "have touched the governor's tenderness," and they predicted he would go soft on these two criminals—which he did. He commuted both their sentences to life in prison. A Winston-Salem minister sent the governor a telegram: "I am sorry to learn that your backbone was too weak to support the decision of the courts." But the governor said, "I cannot contemplate with approval that this woman, unworthy and blackened by sin though she be, shall be shrouded in the cerements of death, dragged along the fatal corridor and bound in the chair of death....This may arise from misconceived sentimentality; it may arise from the deep instincts of the race." In sending Ida to prison for life, he felt honor-bound to handle Sam's appeal in the same manner.

Ida worked in the prison clothing plant. She was released in 1931 and went to work as a laundress at the YWCA. Sam was released the same year.

WINSTON'S WRONGED LOVER

In 1925, author Theodore Dreiser's novel *An American Tragedy* was published. He based his book on the murder of Grace Brown by her lover Chester Gillette, who'd lured her out in a rowboat for a romantic rendezvous on a lake in New York's Adirondack Mountains. Grace worked in Chester's uncle's sewing factory, and Chester had been enjoying Grace's company without ever intending to get himself tied down. He aspired to find a young woman of better social rank and prospects than millworker Grace—though she'd proven fun for a time. But when he met the girl of his ambitious dreams, getting rid of Grace—permanently—was the only way he could see to make a clear path for his new courtship.

Dreiser's fictional account became the basis of the 1951 movie *A Place in the Sun*, starring Elizabeth Taylor and Montgomery Clift. Unfortunately, crime history offers too many tales of women killed by boyfriends because they found a brighter prospect or because what had started as a game turned serious once the girl became pregnant.

In 1892, Winston-Salem saw a version of this sad, too-common tale play out, with some quirks of its own. On Wednesday, July 20, in a grove of trees near the ornate Hotel Zinzendorf, the body of seventeen-year-old Ellen Smith was found. The newspaper identified her as a "white girl...whose character was considered questionable." Ellen had been employed as a cook at Kenny Rose's house on Fifth Street, where she also lodged. According to a detailed post by historian Fam Brownlee for the Forsyth County Central Library's North Carolina Room blog, Ellen started working for Rose—a clerk at one of the city's largest department stores—when she arrived in Winston-Salem from Yadkin County in 1889.

Postcard from Winston-Salem's Hotel Zinzendorff. *From the author's collection; photo by E. Dickinson.*

She worked for him for more than two years and then left in December 1891, reportedly to go back home to have a baby. She returned to her cook's job a few months later, in May 1892. Rose described her as "not bright," but her cooking skills were apparently sufficient.

On July 19, 1892, Ellen left work to buy a yellow silk handkerchief at a store in town and traveled by electric streetcar to West End. Witnesses saw her heading toward the "pleasure ground," the woods behind the commanding Zinzendorf. The hotel would go up in flames a few months later, on Thanksgiving Day 1892, but the wooded park continued to attract visitors and courting couples. Ellen was seen talking to a young man; one passerby said she was sitting with the man's head in her lap. There was nothing unusual about the couple to draw much notice.

The next morning, on a hot Wednesday, a well-dressed young man wearing a brown suit and black derby hat approached Hattie Pratt, a laundress at the Hotel Zinzendorf. He told her he'd found a body in the woods and that she needed to go see it, see if she could identify it. Hattie went only because the young man agreed to go with her, though he slipped away and left her to the task. Hattie described finding a white apron tied onto a bush and the body lying on its face nearby, already swollen with flies buzzing around.

The bullet hole and the powder burns from a shot fired at close range were easy to see on her dress. Suicide seemed unlikely, since a search found no gun nearby. Others summoned to the scene remembered seeing a nattily dressed young man in a suit, but at first, no one could give him a name. One of those who first arrived took the apron from the bush and put it over the girl's head as a sign of respect. Had it been tied on the bush near the pathway through the woods to make the spot easier to find?

The girl's body yielded one clue: in her pocket was a letter from Peter DeGraff (sometimes spelled DeGraf) inviting Ellen to rendezvous with him at that spot in the woods. From the letter, it seemed the couple needed to discuss a disagreement they'd had recently.

The autopsy found that Ellen Smith died from a single gunshot wound. The bullet entered below her left arm and exited to the right after passing through her liver and the body's largest vein just below the heart.

Investigators and the coroner's jury didn't take long to put the pieces of the puzzle together. From the descriptions, some believed the well-dressed young man in the derby hat was Peter DeGraff. Plenty of folks knew that Peter and Ellen had been keeping company, starting in January 1890, soon after she first arrived in Winston-Salem. When she'd left town to spend a few months at her family home in Yadkin County, the timing suggested it was to have Peter DeGraff's baby. The baby didn't live long, and she returned to work in Winston-Salem.

ELLEN SMITH.

Drawing of Ellen Smith by unnamed newspaper artist, sketched from a photograph. *Courtesy of the Winston-Salem Western Sentinel, February 8, 1894.*

The more people officials questioned, the worse the case looked against DeGraff. He'd called on Ellen at the Rose house, and the couple were heard arguing. Peter threatened to shoot her. Witnesses said he visited a local bar the afternoon Ellen was killed, bought some liquor and walked "across the Hanes field in the direction of the fatal spot."

The *Union-Republican* paper offered details about Peter DeGraff from those who knew him: he was "about 25 years old, low in [stature], dark hair and mustache, wears good clothes. He…was born and raised here, was always head strong and unruly and withal a pretty tough boy." According to others, "He has no particular trade or profession, and from boyhood has led a reckless life, drinking,

PETER DEGRAFF.

Drawing of Peter DeGraff by unnamed newspaper artist, sketched from a photograph. *Courtesy of the Winston-Salem Western Sentinel, February 8, 1894.*

gambling, carousing, sporting deadly weapons and bad habits generally, with an especial fondness for the opposite sex…generally to their sorrow."

He'd once tended bar and had been implicated—but not charged—in the Smith-Goins murders in Winston-Salem a year earlier. In May 1891, two groups of men were drinking at a local establishment when some disagreement developed. As the insults and antagonism continued and the groups moved from one drinking spot to another, the anger escalated. Mary Goins, the wife of a tavern owner, was shot by a "young man with straw hat and light suit" as he took aim at one of the other drunken men. John Smith was also caught in the crossfire when his drinking buddy Wilburn Walker pulled out his gun. Both Goins and Smith were killed.

Walker was arrested for a time but released. The man who shot Mary Goins was never clearly identified, and the murders remained unsolved. Plenty of rumors circulated that the well-dressed man was Peter DeGraff, known for his suits and his hats, but officials lacked enough evidence to charge him.

When Ellen died—a year after the Smith and Goins murders—the course of justice wasted no time. On Thursday, July 21, the coroner's jury deliberated and issued the warrant for Peter DeGraff's arrest.

As he'd done after the Goins and Smith shootings, suspect Peter DeGraff went on the run. The newspapers dutifully reported Sheriff Teague's attempts to locate him, including offering $25 of his own money as a reward (worth over $800 today). The previous man in office, Sheriff Boyer, reportedly also "did all in his power" to solve the Goins-Smith case. The *Union Republican* noted that with those three murders in Winston-Salem unsolved, "a blot stands against the good name of our county until the guilty parties in both cases are brought to justice."

By mid-August, a war of words had erupted between rival Winston-Salem newspapers. The *Twin-City Daily Sentinel* took the *Union Republican* to task for an editorial, "a piece of folly to defend the indefensible." News reports of various sightings of Peter DeGraff appeared in the papers, but the *Republican* asserted that Peter had left the area and no one had seen him. According to the *Sentinel*, though, it was a "silly" statement to make because Sheriff Teague had sent posses to search around town. The *Sentinel* held that if DeGraff was gone, then "the sheriff is an ass," and if he's still in the area, "the sheriff is a coward, and negligent in the most culpable degree."

In a move that presaged how newspaper reporters and editors would play detective during the tabloid wars in 1920s and 1930s New York, the *Sentinel* announced that its owner and city editor patrolled Winston-Salem's streets for three hours, starting at the site where Ellen's body was found. They questioned people along the way about what they'd observed. They learned Peter DeGraff had been seen in the area after the murder. He had talked to people he knew from his time as a barkeeper, explaining how he'd told the sheriff he'd meet him at a specified spot but "he didn't propose to be hunted down by a mob."

The flowery exchanges between the newspapers dwindled as time passed, and Peter DeGraff remained missing. Eventually, on July 23, 1893, a year after the murder, officers captured Peter DeGraff in a house next door to the store where'd he purchased liquor the day Ellen died. His arrest shared headlines with Lizzie Borden's acquittal in her Massachusetts trial.

Peter angrily and loudly protested his innocence and told his jailers to keep reporters and preachers away from him. He swore to his mother he hadn't killed anyone.

His trial began on August 11, 1893. Ellen's large family didn't abandon their girl; her aunt Rosa hired lawyers to help prosecute the case—a practice not unheard of at the time but one that cost the farming family substantial money. Her aunt sat on the front row, listening to every word of evidence.

As the state's last piece of evidence, a lawyer read the note found in Ellen's pocket; this strongest piece of evidence against DeGraff was quoted in the *Western Sentinel* (reprinted as written):

> *July 18th, 1892:—Dear Miss Ellen i write this to you to see if you are mad with me. If you are let me know. Pleas Don't thin hard of me for i have love you all my life and can't let nobody but you, so please let me prove your love, Peter DeGraff. So I want you to come tomorrow to the spring if you will pleas come and don't fail for i want you to come good by love. Want to kiss for you * * * * * * as you have done before. P. D. A. f.* [The stars were in the note.]

At the end of the three-day trial, the jurors took eight hours to deliberate before convicting Peter DeGraff, finding "with force and arms and…of his malice aforethought, unlawfully, willfully and feloniously did kill and murder Ellen Smith." The judge sentenced him to hang.

Peter continued to assert his innocence. After months of vehemently refusing counsel from all the city's pastors, at the twelfth hour, he confessed to the First Baptist Church's Reverend H.A. Brown. Standing on the scaffold, after Reverend Brown read scripture and led the crowd in singing "Am I a Soldier of the Cross," Peter admitted his guilt to those gathered: "My hands have been stained in blood." He said he was drunk, that Ellen had been "following him around and would not stop." He said he went back the next day to make sure her body was found quickly. And he warned those who had come to see him die: "I again say to the people here, beware of bad women and whiskey."

According to Fam Brownlee's blog, the *Western Sentinel* delayed its weekly publication in order to report on the hanging and placed the story on the front page, which was usually reserved for national rather than local news. Peter DeGraff was buried within yards of Ellen Smith's grave. The site of the scaffold and the graves are now hidden underneath North Liberty Street, close to Fairchild Road and the runway at Smith Reynolds Airport.

THE PERSONAL AD TRAGEDY

In January 1988, the *Greensboro News & Record* published an upbeat feel-good story that also served as an endorsement for the newspaper's classified ads. Douglas Basham, a bachelor living in Rockingham County, had taken out a personal ad in November 1987:

"D/W/M seeks long lasting loving relationship with a female, 25-35. Me-35. Beard, caring, loving, country boy at heart! You—Special in your own way. Take the chance to write, you might be surprised! Photo please."

120. Personals

DWM Seeks Long Lasting Loving Relationship With a Female 25-35. Me-35. Beard, Caring, Loving, Country Boy At Heart! You-Special In Your Own Way. Take The Chance To Write, You Might Be Surprised! Photo Please. Send To The Ledger P.O. Box 645-35. Eden, N.C. 27288.

Douglas Basham's personal ad as it appeared in the *Greensboro News & Record Ledger.*

His ad was the only one in the classifieds that Sunday looking for love. In those days, long before internet dating and in a place not convenient for casual meetups at coffee shops, he'd placed ads before but hadn't found the lasting love he hoped for. His sister worked at the newspaper, and she encouraged him to set his reluctance aside and try again. It was a small investment that could bring a big return, she said.

His ad appeared the Sunday before Thanksgiving. He got six responses, wrote replies to each one and included his phone number. Only Vivian Hicks contacted him. In Robin Adams's article in the January 4 *News & Record*, Douglas detailed their whirlwind romance: "Then she called me back later that day, and we planned to meet for lunch the following Wednesday. Every [*sic*] since then, I've been on cloud nine. It all happened so fast. I'm just above cloud nine. I've never been this happy in my life. I was shocked that this ad worked. Boy, was I surprised." Douglas said he placed the ad because "I'm just a quiet, lonely boy looking for a nice person."

During that interview, given about six weeks after his ad appeared, he was carrying a laminated copy of it in his pocket. He announced that he and Vivian were planning a wedding for later in January.

Vivian had never answered an ad before, she said, but something about "him being a country boy and saying I could be special in my own way" sparked something. "So I just decided to write and see if he was for real." Vivian had reason to read personal ads, even if she didn't respond to them—her father, she said, met his fourth wife through a personal ad.

The good-news story didn't carry over into January and the new year.

To Douglas's surprise, he learned Vivian Hicks was already married to someone else. She'd taken out a warrant against that husband on December 23, accusing him of threatening "that she would not live to see it" if she continued her divorce proceeding against him. The judge dismissed the charge as "frivolous and malicious" and charged Vivian fifty-two dollars in court costs.

With those revelations, Douglas called off his engagement to Vivian and the wedding plans were canceled.

In February, Douglas got another surprise when police arrested him. Vivian claimed that Douglas was beating her and harassing her with telephone calls. "He got so possessive, I couldn't even breathe," she told reporter Janice Heller. "I couldn't marry someone who would be so possessive of me. I had to carry him to court. He left me alone after that." Based on her charges, Douglas was arrested on February 10.

On February 23, while Douglas was awaiting trial on the assault and harassment charges, Vivian officially dropped her divorce suit against her current husband.

On March 29, Rockingham County's District Court found Douglas innocent of her two charges against him. That should have ended the drama of the whirlwind romance and the convoluted court proceedings. But two months after his court victory, Douglas's sister got a phone call that her brother was dead. The caller didn't give a name.

Deputies found Douglas's body in his trailer near the Bethany School in rural Rockingham County. As he sat in a chair in his living room drawing on a notepad, someone standing outside on his patio shot him once right between the eyes with a rifle. His glasses were broken in two pieces. When the sheriff's deputies responded, they found Douglas sitting with a pen in his hand, his television on and the washing machine running.

At first, the investigation led nowhere. Vivian Hicks was naturally someone investigators questioned. She denied knowing anything about his death and told the news reporter, "I really hate that it happened." The county's district attorney felt they'd reached an impasse in questioning Vivian and was ready to devote resources to finding other leads, but Sheriff's Detective Sam Page had a "gut feeling" about Vivian and kept pushing.

On June 23, 1988, Vivian Hicks, age thirty-three, and Michael Alvin Scales, age twenty-one and identified as her current boyfriend, were arrested and charged with Douglas's murder. She'd met Michael at Sparky's Food Store, where she worked. They at first denied that they were dating, but Michael obviously felt protective of her. He quickly confessed to shooting Douglas, saying Vivian had asked for his help, that Douglas was beating her and she "needed to get rid of him."

After the shooting, he'd hidden the .243-caliber deer-hunting rifle at his grandmother's house in Virginia for a while. Then he brought it home and tossed it in the Mayo River, off the road near U.S. 220. He tried to guide officers to where he'd thrown it, but they never located the gun. The sheriff wanted the weapon to round out the case, but they had enough to move forward with prosecution.

In court Michael and Vivian both pleaded not guilty, but in a signed statement during the investigation, Michael had admitted he committed the murder. "I pulled the trigger. I think I was loving her so much….I guess I thought I would put a stop to it and give her a little peace. I ain't never in my life thought about killing nobody."

Rockingham County Courthouse in Wentworth, which now houses the county museum and archives. *Photo courtesy of Indy beetle via Wikimedia Commons.*

Vivian Hicks maintained that Michael acted on his own, that she had nothing to do with it. However, just over a month after their arrests, both Vivian and Michael entered guilty pleas to first-degree murder and received mandatory life sentences, which at the time allowed for the possibility of parole after twenty years. The district attorney's assessment of the circumstances didn't allow for a death-penalty prosecution, but the two defendants accepted the maximum punishment they could have received at trial. Exactly why they pleaded guilty without gaining some benefit in sentencing wasn't clear to those reporting on the proceedings.

Because Vivian never gave a detailed statement about what happened, her motives were never clear. She was married but also shopping the personal ads. She started a divorce but then turned on Douglas, a man she said was treating her well and made claims of stalking and abuse that she didn't provide evidence to support in court. And once the two seemed shed of each other, she decided Douglas needed to be killed and inveigled a young man into taking care of it for her. What prompted all the tragic drama? Was her life lived in some contorted soap opera? Over thirty years later, the answers aren't any clearer, but lonely couples now look for love on online dating apps. Some find what they're looking for. Some find a nightmare.

4
BLACK WIDOWS—AND
A WIDOWER

BARBARA STAGER

Rarely do ex-wives help solve the murders of their former husbands. Rarer still is a case where that ex-wife helps reopen the case of another of the black widow's victims. But in North Carolina, an ex-wife did just that, making sure a murderous second wife was sentenced for one murder and connected to another.

The story started in 1978, in Trinity, North Carolina, south of High Point in Randolph County, population seven thousand. Barbara Ford asked her preacher to go with her to obtain a gun permit; her husband, Larry, had encouraged her to buy a small .25-caliber pistol for protection, she said. A coworker went with her to buy the gun and took her out to a wooded area behind an old farmhouse to make sure she knew how to shoot it. He covered the safety points of the automatic and warned her that the gun could fire even without the loaded clip inserted, that a round could already be in the chamber and ready to fire.

Later that same day, on March 22, 1978, Larry Ford came home from his regular karate class. He complained of a painful kick to the groin and went straight upstairs to bed. Barbara decided to sleep on the couch so she wouldn't disturb him. That night, a sound woke her, and she went to check on him. He was gasping for breath and the gun she'd just purchased was in the bed beside him. She later told family members that the medical examiner, because he found no gunshot residue on Larry's hands, surmised Larry had dropped the gun and it fired accidentally. That remained Barbara's version of the story.

Her version omitted details observed by the EMTs who responded to her 911 call that night. When they'd arrived, Barbara told them she thought he shot himself while cleaning the gun for her. They found the automatic pistol's clip under the bed covers. The gun was found beside his right hip. He had blood on the front of his pajamas. The bullet had entered his chest; he'd died only minutes before the EMTs arrived. An EMT saw a gun cleaning rod with the gun's box on top of the chest of drawers in the bedroom, but he saw no gun-cleaning oil or wipe cloths. The purchase receipt showed she'd bought the gun at 3:35 that afternoon. By midnight, the sheriff's deputy had arrived to investigate.

With questions about how the clip had ejected from the gun and landed under the covers, how the gun had fallen where they found it and Barbara's unusual lack of emotion, one of the EMTs called his EMS director. When the director arrived, he also found Barbara "wasn't exactly very upset about the whole situation," according to later testimony.

Before the body was removed for autopsy, Larry's hands were bagged to preserve evidence. The forensic chemist at the SBI found no gunshot residue on his hands. The amount of residue released varies with individual handguns, but test-fires of this gun produced "significantly high concentrations of gunshot residue." Tests also showed the gun drop-fired when it hit a hard tile floor from a height of at least five feet. The state's firearm examiner didn't believe the story that it accidentally fired when dropped from a shorter distance onto a carpeted floor or a mattress.

Despite all the questions surrounding the case, investigators couldn't get clear-cut answers and no charges were filed. Larry Ford's handwritten will left their $40,000 house and its contents to Barbara. Insurance companies were reluctant to pay, but she eventually collected over $70,000 on two policies despite the suspicions. She later received almost $50,000 in an additional payment after the sheriff's office declared Larry Ford's case closed.

By the fall of 1978, Barbara Terry Ford had moved to Durham and met tall, athletic Russ Stager, who taught and coached at Durham High School. The couple married months later, on March 17, 1979—a year after Larry's death. Russ adopted Larry's and Barbara's two sons, aged ten and four. The couple were active church members and well-known in the community. Less widely known were the deepening fractures in the marriage. Unexpected for a girl raised as a churchgoing Baptist, Barbara

The old Durham High School building originally opened in 1922. *Courtesy of Warren LeMay via Wikimedia Commons.*

maintained an active extracurricular sex life. During both of her marriages, her multiple affairs caused problems. At least as difficult for her husbands were her crazy spending habits. Whether in bed or at the shopping mall, Barbara seemed insatiable.

During her nine-year marriage to Russ, the couple had climbed out of a couple of seriously deep financial holes. Russ was, after all, a high school teacher and coach—not the highest paid of professions. Barbara worked in real estate, at banks and other office jobs—or she said she did. They lived much better than others with such modest means. Some close to the couple knew Russ had struggled to get their debt under control, but according to court records, Barbara's spending again escalated by January 1987. For a while, Russ too enjoyed the bigger houses, Rolex watches, clothes and cars—according to one of her sons, twenty cars in nine years, including a Cadillac and a Mercedes. And a couple of boats.

Barbara was adept at the sophisticated shell game of hiding the debts from Russ. She kited checks between bank accounts, forged Russ's name on loan applications and a car title in order to obtain loans, hid bills from him when they arrived or diverted the mail to her parents' house. She'd also been working for a local radio station and owed the station almost

$3,000 for unearned commissions. When the station manager told Russ she didn't work there anymore, he said Russ became "very emotional and teary-eyed."

As the house of credit grew more unstable, she announced some exciting news: a New York publisher had just accepted her book, *Untimely Death*, based on Larry Ford's death. She waived around a letter from Doubleday, offering her a $400,000 advance on her book royalties. Disaster averted. Based on that letter, she took out a $10,000 bank loan to pay off some debt. Things were looking up for Barbara and her heavy spending habits.

But she kept spending and kept having extramarital liaisons.

Then, another 911 call. On February 1, 1988, just after six o'clock in the morning, Durham County sheriff's deputies were called to the house Russ and Barbara shared. They found him dead in the couple's bed. Russ's adopted fourteen-year-old son—Larry Ford's son—had made the 911 call for his mother. She'd told him his father had been shot. Sergeant Rick Buchanan of the Durham County Sheriff's Office became the investigative lead in the case.

First responders found Russ barely alive, lying on his left side facing the center of the bed with his face partially hidden by the pillow. They moved his head so he could breathe more easily and revealed a .25-caliber Beretta pistol. Under the pillow, they found a spent shell casing from the gun. He'd been shot once in the back of the head. He was taken to the hospital, where he later died without regaining consciousness.

Meanwhile, investigators were questioning Barbara. When the first officer arrived, he found her sitting on the edge of the bed where her husband lay. He reported that she wore blue jeans, a sweatshirt and tennis shoes; her appearance was neat. One responder noted "a slight indication of crying but very little."

She kept repeating how much she hated guns, how she hated that Russ kept guns, that she was scared of guns. She said Russ was afraid someone would break into the house, and he sometimes slept with a handgun under his pillow, which frightened her. She'd heard her youngest son get up to go to the bathroom, and she feared Russ would think he was a burglar. She reached over to pull the gun out from under the pillow and it went off. She'd killed him. She hadn't meant to. She was so sorry.

One of the EMTs attended church with Russ and Barbara and with Russ's parents. He offered to call his parents or the church pastor as the ambulance took Russ to Duke Medical Center. Barbara didn't want him to call anyone, which he found odd.

On occasion, a couple can become genuine friends after a divorce. That was the story of Jo Lynn Snow and Russ Stager, her first husband—a mutual affection hard-won following their divorce. "We worked better as friends," she said. That friendship was why Russ confided in Jo Lynn in July 1984, almost four years before his 1988 death. Jo Lynn told *Raleigh News & Observer* reporter Anne Blythe that Russ said, "I'm probably being paranoid, but if anything ever happens to me, will you please look into it?" This cryptic but serious plea came five years after his marriage to his second wife, Barbara.

Jo Lynn took the promise she made to her ex-husband Russ seriously. In the process, she also found herself committed to finding the truth for Larry Ford, Barbara's first husband. On February 2, the day after Russ's death, Jo Lynn met with Detective Rick Buchanan and handed him a letter she'd taken time to write; she wanted to make sure she didn't forget anything. Knowing what she knew, Jo Lynn was surprised to learn they hadn't ordered an autopsy on Russ Stager. She outlined Russ's concerns, Barbara's rumored affairs, the money troubles, that Russ was a longtime member of the Army Reserves and never treated guns with anything but caution. She also made sure Rick Buchanan knew about Larry Ford, how he'd died and the insurance proceeds from his death.

After Russ's funeral, given what he was learning about Larry Ford's death, Rick Buchanan asked Barbara if she would reenact Russ's shooting for him. As he later told author Jerry Bledsoe, "I can't imagine somebody crawling back up in this same bed where her spouse was just shot and killed by her own hand and going through it again. I can't imagine it." But she did—and she allowed the investigators to film it. The video later turned this case into television true crime gold. As she moved around on the bed and realized that what she was acting out didn't quite work with what she'd described, she kept altering her story. That reenactment led to her arrest.

In December 1988, another surprise turn in the case surfaced. Ten months after Russ's death, a student found a cassette tape under lockers in Coach Stager's old office at Durham High School. The student took it to his mother, but she put it aside and didn't listen to it until four months later, in April—only weeks before the murder trial began. On the tape, Russ Stager's voice detailed his concerns about his wife's behavior. According to court records, Russ made the tape three days before he died. On it, he said he was afraid of his wife, that she'd been waking him up recently to give him what she said was aspirin. She was insistent, so he'd managed to look as if he'd taken them but hid them instead. The pharmacist at Eckerd's told him they were sleeping pills, not aspirin.

Russ related on the tape that Barbara's first husband had died of a gunshot wound, but he didn't know the details and didn't know what to believe about that incident. According to court records, he said,

> *The first one, I don't know what happened but according to his parents there was some foul play going on. He supposedly, accidentally shot himself in their bedroom with a pistol. Now, I have no idea what really went on, what really happened. She was there when it happened and so were the boys. My question is did her husband, Larry Ford, accidentally shoot himself?…I'm just being paranoid about all this stuff. Sometimes I wonder.*

His list of her questionable actions continued. He talked about finding her parked at the county stadium apparently "making out" with another man. She turned the incident on him, saying it was because he "wasn't giving her affection." He said police came to the house with warrants for unpaid bills. At her bank job, she'd gotten in trouble for diverting money from a customer's loan payment; Russ had repaid some of that. They were denied a loan at another bank because of some trouble in her past that he never fully understood. Bills kept not arriving at their home when expected, so he'd gotten a post office box and kept the key so he could check it, but Barbara repeatedly took the key off his ring to go check the mail. She said she'd called Visa to locate missing bills.

Lee County Courthouse. *Courtesy of North Carolina Judicial Branch.*

His words on the tape poured out a litany of unsolved financial mysteries and lies and forgery, spoken by a man who was finally facing reality. At one point, he said, "I really hope that I'm being paranoid about all this stuff that's going on, but I really wonder. This is…Russ Stager…uh…this is January 29, 1988, ten minutes of two."

Three days later, Russ Stager was dead. In the weeks before his death, he'd been putting the puzzle pieces together and doing what he could to prevent another meltdown in the family's finances. He had a moment of hope, with Barbara's new publishing contract, but as the prosecution would later argue, some key pieces were hidden, and Barbara Stager couldn't afford for him to find them—especially that the publishing contract and the huge advance were elaborate lies.

On April 18, 1988, Barbara was arrested at her dream house on Fox Drive.

Her defense team asked for a change of venue, moving the trial from Durham County to Lee County in Sanford because of the heavy publicity.

The jury deliberated only forty-four minutes before finding her guilty. She was sentenced to death. On appeal in 1991, she argued that the death of her first husband, Larry Ford, and Russ's tape recording and other evidence shouldn't have been admitted. The North Carolina Supreme Court held that allowing evidence about Larry's shooting death was admissible, that it didn't unfairly prejudice her case but instead responded to her claims that she hadn't fired guns and was afraid of them. Larry's death also shared clear similarities with Russ Stager's. Citing existing case law, the court said, "The fortuitous coincidence becomes too abnormal, bizarre, implausible, unusual, or objectively improbable to be believed. The coincidence becomes telling evidence of mens rea," translated as "guilty mind" or the knowledge or intent that actions are wrong.

The court upheld the admission of that evidence but ultimately overturned the death penalty on a technicality involving how jurors may have interpreted a mitigating factor question. On resentencing, she was given a natural life sentence, which at the time gave her the possibility of parole.

The case attracted international interest, long before cable news true crime became a twenty-four-hour-a-day staple. In 1994, North Carolina native and crime journalist Jerry Bledsoe published *Before He Wakes*, the definitive book on the case. Television accounts have aired on *Forensic Files*, *Scorned: Love Kills*, *City Confidential*, *American Justice* and *New Detectives*, among others. To date, her parole requests have been denied, and at age seventy-five, she continues to serve her sentence in North Carolina's women's prison.

BETTY LOU BEETS

Sometimes North Carolinians don't stay in North Carolina to commit their crimes. Sometimes they move and their crimes become linked with another state, but no matter how far away they go, news reports identify them as "born in North Carolina."

Betty Lou Dunevant Beets is linked with Texas because that's where she committed her crimes and where her life ended, but she was born in Roxboro, North Carolina, close to the Virginia border. Her father's job moved them over the state line to Virginia when Betty was young. By the time she was twelve years old, her mother had been institutionalized, and Betty had the responsibility of caring for her younger siblings while her father worked industrial jobs.

A childhood case of measles left her with a hearing impairment. Life wasn't easy for the oldest child in the Dunevant family, but could that explain the path her life took? At age fifteen, Betty escaped her family by marrying Robert Branson in 1953. They stayed married for sixteen years and had five children, but Branson left the family in 1969.

Betty's first marriage was her longest in a series of six (twice to one man). Months after her first husband left, she and Billy York Lane married

Postcard of downtown Roxboro, photographed circa 1930–45. *Courtesy of Boston Public Library, Tichnor Brothers Collection.*

in 1970. This relationship was no bed of roses—Betty was charged with attempted murder for shooting Billy, but the charges were dropped when he admitted he broke her nose and threatened to kill her. The couple divorced after two years.

After that split, Betty remained single for about six years. Even as she got older, she could still attract men. In 1978, she married Ronnie Threlkeld, but again, evidence of marital discord soon appeared on the police blotter. This time, she tried, unsuccessfully, to run Ronnie down with a car.

Her fourth husband, Wayne Barker, disappeared in 1981, months after the couple married.

In 1983, her fifth husband, Jimmy Don Beets, disappeared from their Texas home, eleven months after their marriage. On August 6, Betty got a phone call from Lil Smith, the owner of the Redwood Beach Marina on Cedar Creek Reservoir. Some of her customers had spotted an empty boat floating near the dock. They retrieved it and found Jimmy Don's fishing license inside. Lil Smith first called the Coast Guard and the Parks and Wildlife officials, and then she called Jimmy Don's house several times before Betty answered.

The boat's propeller was missing, but his nitroglycerin heart medication was on board. Had he had a heart attack and fallen into the water? Severe weather prevented searches from starting until the next day, August 7. They could find no sign of Jimmy Don, even after three weeks spent dragging the lake near Gun Barrel City.

Jimmy Don Beets was a captain with the Dallas Fire Department, and the fire department's chaplain visited to console and counsel Betty during the weeks of searching. She asked him if she was entitled to any benefits under Jimmy Don's insurance or retirement plan. The chaplain checked for her and was glad he could report back that she was beneficiary of a $110,000 life insurance policy and could collect $1,200 a month from his pension. Unfortunately, unless Jimmy Don's body was found, she'd have to wait seven years before he could be declared legally dead and the benefits activated.

The search for Jimmy Don went cold after law enforcement exhausted all leads. But the lack of new leads didn't tamp down the rumors. Betty bartended at a local club. People knew she'd had at least three other husbands. Sheriff's investigator Rick Rose said he'd heard "considerable speculation" that Jimmy Don had been murdered.

Betty, though, wasn't talking to law enforcement.

Two years later, in 1985, the sheriff's investigator got an anonymous phone call from a "credible confidential source" telling him where the bodies were buried. He later told a UPI reporter that the caller was remarkably accurate in describing the locations, "within three or four inches."

A search of the Beets property located Jimmy Don buried under a decorative wishing well that he'd built for Betty in the front yard. She'd planted flowers over the body.

As the anonymous caller had said, the searchers also found the body of husband no. 4, Wayne Barker, buried under a storage shed behind the garage. Both were wrapped in sleeping bags. The Dallas medical examiner determined that both men had been shot, two or three times each, and could have been shot with the same .38-caliber pistol, though none of the experts could conclusively state that it was fired from the collector's item pistol found in Betty's house.

Much testimony surrounded whether and how she tried to get money from Jimmy Don's estate—from selling a house he owned, his fire department insurance policy, his pension and other sources.

At trial, Jimmy Don's niece, who worked for J.C. Penney Life Insurance Company, told how he'd canceled a $10,000 life insurance policy taken out without his permission. The application had arrived in the J.C. Penney department store bill, but the address on the completed application belonged to one of Betty's daughters. Betty admitted she signed the application herself. She had also forged the bill of sale for Jimmy Don's boat.

Betty's treachery extended beyond how she treated her husbands. When confronted with the deaths of two husbands and the attacks on two others, Betty responded by blaming two of her children. She said she suspected son Robbie, in separate incidents, of hot-wiring Jimmy Don's boat, breaking the propeller, getting the truck tires muddy, stealing Jimmy Don's money from a whiskey bottle and shooting him in the bedroom. Betty admitted that she helped Robbie bury him, after her youngest son, Bobby, had fallen asleep in their house trailer.

In addition to burying Jimmy Don, she'd also gotten her son to plant the heart medicine on the abandoned boat. Daughter Shirley didn't actively participate, but she knew about her mother's plans to kill Jimmy Don and she helped dispose of Doyle Wayne Barker's body in the backyard.

Betty assured her son that if anyone found out, he was to say nothing and she would take the blame—a pledge she didn't honor.

Betty's testimony often veered into odd side issues. She testified that "I could never hurt Jimmy Don….I loved Jimmy Don. Nobody's ever been as good to me as he was." She said she'd tried to take care of him, even though he appeared dead. She pulled the bedsheet up over him and told him "as if he were still alive, he must understand that to protect Robbie, they must bury him in their front yard." She made a point about Beets's burial as if it was important—that they "put it into the planter. It wasn't a wishing well."

Betty, age forty-eight, was arrested the same day the remains of her husbands were uncovered, before they were officially identified. She was charged with capital murder in the deaths of Jimmy Don Beets and Wayne Barker. Her $1 million bail was the equivalent of more than $2.5 million today. Shirley was also charged and held with the same bail.

At her trial, Betty's son Robbie put all the pieces together for the jury. He testified that his mother asked him to leave the house, that she intended to kill Jimmy Don. Robbie said he stayed away for two hours, came home and found Betty with the body. The two of them made use of the wishing well Jimmy Don had built for her. Robbie also placed the nitroglycerin pills on the boat, abandoned it in the lake, and caught a ride home with his mother. Betty's defense attorney asked if it wasn't true that Robbie was the killer, not his mother, but Robbie's testimony didn't waver.

Betty's daughter Shirley also knew beforehand parts of Betty's plans to kill Jimmy Don. The original plan was to dump his body off the boat into the lake, and Shirley didn't learn until later about the wishing well. Back in October 1981, Shirley also knew that Betty planned to kill Wayne Barker, that "she couldn't put up with anymore of him beating her and that she didn't want him around anymore." Wayne owned the house trailer where they lived, and in a divorce, Betty would lose it.

Shirley testified that, after her mother shot the sleeping Wayne Barker, she helped drag his body to the backyard where Betty had a hole dug for a barbecue pit. Instead of a barbecue, Betty got Shirley to help her build a new patio with some cinder blocks. Later, a shed was put on top of the patio.

In October 1985, the jury found Betty guilty of killing Jimmy Don Beets for "remuneration," a point much debated in her appeal. She was sentenced to death by lethal injection.

Betty apparently thought she would benefit from Jimmy Don's retirement benefits and life insurance policies, though she specifically denied that she'd killed him for money. That, after all, was the aggravating factor that made her case death-penalty eligible. The appellate court debated the state's death penalty statute and what "for remuneration" meant. Was it intended only to make hired killers eligible for the death penalty? The court decided "remuneration" also included expecting to benefit from insurance or other estate proceeds as a result of a murder.

Betty never admitted to killing Jimmy Don—the only murder she was convicted of committing—or Wayne Barker.

Texas was not a state known for any sentimentality or reluctance about prosecuting women—or sentencing them to death. Her trial attracted plenty of reporters, but opposition to her death sentence made even bigger international headlines.

The trail of marriages and violence in Betty's life began in her small-town upbringing in North Carolina. With her claims of sexual and physical abuse dating back to childhood, her crimes and the fight for her life made her one of the most recognized female killers in the United States. According to reporter Geraldine Sealy, in the years between 1991 and Betty's execution, courts commuted the sentences of more than one hundred battered women. In Betty's case, though, the jury wasn't presented evidence of a history of battery or domestic violence.

Despite the media attention, legal appeals, advocacy by groups representing battered women, death-penalty opponents and pleas for a stay of execution to the Texas governor and to the U.S Supreme Court, Betty Lou Beets, age sixty-two, died by lethal injection in Huntsville, Texas, on February 24, 2000. She was the first woman executed in the new millennium and the second executed in Texas since the Civil War; the first was Karla Faye Tucker in 1998, who killed two victims with a pickaxe.

TIM BOCZKOWSKI

Most murders are, statistically, committed by someone who won't kill again. Many don't intend to kill the first time. In a few noteworthy cases, though, that first murder leads to another. Perhaps to several others. Like hitting the slots in Vegas, a killer can start to feel lucky. Or charmed. Or smarter than everyone else.

On November 4, 1990, Tim Boczkowski ran to a neighbor's house in North Greensboro for help, reporting that his wife, Elaine, had died in the bathtub. Some thought the circumstances were unusual and certainly tragic. But who believed it could be something as serious as murder?

Thirty-four-year-old Elaine liked to relax in a hot bath in the family's apartment. That night, Tim said he heard a thump from the bathroom, and he found Elaine under the water. He said she'd had too much to drink at a church dance that evening. Oddly though, when investigators arrived, the tub showed no signs of having been filled with water. She had vomited in the tub—Tim said that happened when he tried to resuscitate her. Her body registered no blood alcohol at autopsy, but Tim told the first officer on the scene that his wife "was basically a lush." The medical examiner noted bruises, cracked ribs and marks or bruises across her chest and abdomen. Perhaps, though, those injuries resulted from a fall or from the actions of paramedics trying to save her life. State medical examiner Dr. John Butts ruled the cause and the manner of death as undetermined. The investigators were suspicious of Tim and his version of events, of his struggling ice cream business and Elaine's $25,000 life insurance policy, but they didn't have the evidence to prove murder.

After Elaine's death, Tim Boczkowski moved with his three children—two boys and a girl, ages nine, six and five—to a suburb outside Pittsburgh for a new life and a new job making dentures. He soon met Maryann at a Catholic church gathering. They married in 1993; she adopted the threesome and helped Tim start his new career. Unexpectedly, on November 7, 1994, Allegheny County investigators were called to the Boczkowski house, where they found Maryann dead, lying on the deck beside the family's backyard hot tub—four years and three days after Tim's first wife died in her bathtub in Greensboro.

First responders found Tim trying to resuscitate Maryann on the deck. They noted wet beach towels, a broken temperature gauge on the hot tub and a package for an oral resuscitation shield designed to protect someone giving CPR from exposure to disease, which seemed an odd item to use with a family member. They didn't know about Elaine in North Carolina or the vomit in her bathtub. When they asked about scratches on his neck and back, Tim explained that Maryann had given him a "scratch massage" that evening. Tim also told police that he and Maryann had argued once again about how much she was drinking. The last time he saw her, she was in the hot tub with her wineglass. Drinking had become a real problem for her, he said.

The second tragic loss of a wife was not easy for Tim to explain. Tim's comment as Maryann's body was put in the ambulance stuck with Sergeant Dave Schwab of the Alleghany County Police: "I hope they don't try to put this on me." That wasn't a comment Schwab expected to hear as an initial reaction from a grieving husband. Tim's father was the one who explained to detectives how Tim's first wife, Elaine, had died.

The autopsy revealed that the multiple bruises on Maryann's body were mostly on her back, across the strong strap muscles on either side of her neck and on the inside of her gums and lips. She also had five distinct bruises on her scalp—similar to injuries found on Elaine's scalp. Maryann didn't drown; she died of asphyxia from neck compression. Her blood alcohol was high, at .22, which could make it hard for her to fight off an attack. And Tim was the beneficiary on a $100,000 life insurance policy. According to a TV documentary, he'd used their cash wedding gifts to pay the policy premiums.

Not only were investigators in Pennsylvania skeptical of his story, but now Greensboro detectives had a reason to renew their interest in Elaine's death. Liz Maple, Elaine's friend and neighbor, had kept the children after Tim came to her house that night for help. She told police that, the following morning, the youngest said "he didn't think his Mommy was going to be all right." Through the door of the bathroom, he'd seen his father holding her down in the bathtub.

According to an interview with Linn Thomas of the *Greensboro News & Record*, Elaine had confided in Liz that she was preparing to leave Tim and taking steps to afford to get away with her children. She borrowed suitable interview clothes from Liz and was looking for a secretarial job. In a couple of months, she also expected to collect a large insurance payment from injuries in a car accident.

Greensboro investigators had their suspicions in Elaine's case from the scene that night. Dr. Deborah Radisch from the North Carolina state medical examiner's office said Elaine wasn't drunk, though her husband claimed she was. Elaine had no water in her airways, but that's not always present in a drowning. "Dry drownings" occur in 10 to 15 percent of drowning deaths, caused when a laryngospasm prevents water from entering the lungs. Her death was suspicious, but Dr. Radisch, at that time, said she lacked evidence to refute Tim's claims, finding the cause of death as "undetermined."

Detective Brenda Vance with the Greensboro Police Department had been on the scene as a rookie uniformed officer when they investigated Elaine's death in 1990. Brenda Vance had questions about the scene, convinced that Tim had held his wife over the edge of the tub and cut off her breathing. She saw vomit inside the tub, but no water outside, not even in the tracks for the shower door. Four years later, she was a Greensboro police detective with more experience with crime scenes. She'd done some experiments of her own. As she described for *Forensic Files*, her tub at home was the same size as the Boczkowskis'. She was the same size as Elaine. When she tried to submerge her head in her tub at home, it bobbed above the water and the overflow valve drained the displaced water. What Tim described just didn't make sense.

In light of the new evidence, especially what the children said that night, the medical examiner believed the circumstances supported a finding of homicide as the manner of Elaine's death, that she'd been pushed against the metal shower door track on the side of the tub compressing her chest until she stopped breathing. The cause of death was asphyxiation.

Tim's first trial started on October 21, 1996, at North Carolina's Guilford County Courthouse. The jury sentenced him to life in prison. In appealing his conviction, his attorney argued that the jury should not have heard evidence about his second wife's death, that it was prejudicial. The court held that, under the state's rules of evidence, such testimony could be admitted as long as it wasn't done simply to show the defendant's bad character or his propensity to kill his wives. "It may, however," according to the ruling, "be admissible for other purposes, such as proof of motive, opportunity, intent, preparation, plan, knowledge, identity, or absence of mistake, entrapment or accident." When Tim claimed both deaths were accidents, evidence of both were held admissible because of the similarities.

In its ruling, the court cited the appellate opinion from Barbara Stager's case: "When an accused contends a victim's death was an accident rather

Guilford County Courthouse in Greensboro. *Courtesy of North Carolina Judicial Branch.*

than a homicide, '[e]vidence of similar acts may be offered to show that the act in dispute was not inadvertent, accidental or involuntary.'" Based on the doctrine of chances, "the more often a defendant performs a certain act, the less likely it is that the defendant acted innocently."

Another element in Tim's appeal was whether the jury should have heard what his then-nine-year-old daughter told the church lady who came to help care for the siblings the morning after Elaine died. The girl said she'd heard her parents fighting in the bathroom and her mother saying, "No, Tim, no. Stop." The daughter shared that as the family friend took her upstairs to pack some clothes before they left the apartment. At trial, the daughter denied that she'd said she heard a fight or her mother asking her dad to stop. By the time the case was tried, the children were older and realized they stood to lose their dad if he was convicted—and they'd already lost their mother and a stepmother who'd loved them.

The appellate court upheld the decision to treat the daughter's statement as an "excited utterance" exception to the hearsay rule. "When considering the spontaneity of statements made by young children, there is more flexibility" because of the stress they're experiencing and the reduced likelihood that the statement resulted from reflection or fabrication.

About fifteen years after the death of his mother, son Todd, age six when she died, began training for a law enforcement career. He and his older sister and brother had stood by their dad through his trials and incarceration, but what he was learning in his training raised questions for him. In an interview with Aaron Rasmussen for Investigation Discovery, he said, "Just the unusual circumstances, with both happening around tubs. My stepmother's autopsy showing signs of strangulation. That's tough evidence to refute." He also thinks Maryann started having questions about his father and tried to meet with his father's sister and a friend to get answers. She didn't live long enough to have those conversations.

Because Elaine's murder took place before 1994, Tim was eligible for parole, and North Carolina released him in 2018 after he served twenty-two years. He was delivered directly to Pennsylvania to serve his life sentence for Maryann's murder.

In 1999, a Pennsylvania jury had given him the death penalty, finding as the aggravating factor that he'd killed his first wife in the same way. But he was resentenced in 2004 to life without parole. The appeals court found that the Allegheny County district attorney had violated a judge's order. Boczkowski was to be extradited to North Carolina only after he was first tried in Pennsylvania. Instead, he was first tried and convicted in North

Carolina. That conviction for his first wife's murder provided grounds for him to receive the death penalty in Pennsylvania. As his defense lawyer argued, violating the judge's order meant he ended up with a "murder prone" and "death qualified" jury for his second trial for Maryann's death. The appellate court found it improper to mention the North Carolina conviction in the Pennsylvania case.

After the death penalty was set aside, Tim finally admitted to his son Todd that what he'd seen through the bathroom door when he was five years old was real, that he'd seen him killing his mother. As an adult, Todd had no memory of witnessing that scene or telling the neighbor. Why would Tim admit it fourteen years later? Maybe because he no longer had to lie—the consequences he faced couldn't get any worse.

In her investigation of murdered and missing wives who are "erased" by their spouses, journalist Marilee Strong noted that, while awaiting trial in Pennsylvania, a fellow inmate asked Tim why he'd killed his second wife in basically the same way he'd killed his first. "That was stupid, wasn't it," Tim reportedly responded. His lack of creativity helped convict him—twice. But Strong noted, "What we don't know is how many eraser killers elude detection by murdering just once, establishing no pattern to attract attention."

In 2023, Tim Boczkowski turned sixty-eight years old, still serving his sentence in Pennsylvania.

5
SMALL-TOWN CRIMES

ALMA PETTY

Eleven-year-old boys are notoriously curious—especially in a small town like Reidsville, where they have to make their own fun. On a lazy day in 1928, young Phil Link saw the sheriff down the street from his house outside the Petty home. He later said that wasn't too unusual since Rockingham County sheriff J.F. "Chunk" Smith lived on Lindsey Street, too. But men with shovels and the crowds waiting for a glimpse, that looked like something interesting.

Phil crossed the street and found a dusty basement window where he could check out what was happening inside. He watched as the men shoveled coal off a heap and uncovered a decomposing body. The sight in the basement was gruesome, and as he knelt outside, the smell knocked him off his haunches. He ran home with a story to tell, one he told many times over the years. Fortunately for those interested in crime history, after his retirement as a pharmacist, Phil Link researched and wrote about the murder in the house across the street. Otherwise, the trial of Alma Petty Gatlin for the axe murder of her father could have been one of those tales that hit national headlines and then disappeared from the community's notice, even though it raised interesting questions about the difficulties of deciding which version of a story is the real one and when a confession should be admissible.

Smith Petty was often absent from his family home on Lindsey Street, just off Reidsville's Main Street. He sometimes took work in mills around the area, but he often took drunk benders, so neighbors never knew exactly where he'd gone in the fall of 1926. His family likely was relieved, because a drunken Smith Petty was also a violent Smith Petty, given to beating his wife and children.

After almost six months, people did start wondering when Smith Petty didn't return to attend his wife's funeral. She died of pneumonia following a miscarriage on March 9, 1927. On July 7, his daughter Alma married Eugene Gatlin, the local fire chief, and they set up house. Smith didn't appear for the wedding either.

Months later, in May 1927, Baptist evangelist Thomas "Thunderbolt" Pardue preached a revival sermon in Reidsville. His topic was repentance and "the confession of our sins." Moved by his message, Alma answered the altar call for prayer, then stayed behind after the meeting broke up to speak with the minister. She asked for a private confessional time and suggested they speak in the choir loft, away from others. He didn't believe her when she said she'd committed murder. He certainly didn't believe she'd killed her father.

"How did you do it?"

"It was easy." Just like the Gray-Snyder murders, she said. Ruth Snyder and her lover Judd Gray had set the New York tabloids afire when they bludgeoned Ruth's husband with a window-sash weight and tried to collect his insurance so they could live happily ever after. The case was news at the time, but the circumstances were nothing like what happened in the house on Lindsey Street. The preacher asked what she did with the body. She would say only that she'd put it in her trunk and buried it, but she didn't tell him where.

The minister reported her admission to members of law enforcement, though at first, no one took any action or acted like they believed him.

After repeated visits from Reverend Pardue—the former evangelist who was now pastor of a local church—the Rockingham County solicitor began an investigation in August. The sheriff went to the house where the Pettys had lived but had since vacated. They didn't have to dig deep in the basement to find the body, covered by only a thin layer of red clay. Several neighbors and Smith Petty's physician were called by the coroner to identify the badly decomposed remains.

According to Reverend Pardue, as Alma initially told him the story, one morning, she put cereal on the table for her father and was cooking him an egg for breakfast. He'd beaten her mother the night before, and Alma had hidden an axe behind the kitchen door, just in case. While he sat with his back to her, eating and cussing and threatening her, she hefted the axe and struck him in the back of the head. The coroner's report later said he suffered three blows, any one of which could have killed him.

In breaking the news, the Greensboro paper reported, "To say that the finding of the body and the arrest of Mrs. Gatlin astonished and stunned this city would be putting it mildly."

Evidence showed that her father had indeed been killed with an axe, with the first blow coming from behind him as he sat eating breakfast. She said she hit him on the right side over his ear; the physician confirmed the five-inch wound. She said when he fell to the floor, she struck him again. According to the medical report, the skull was crushed on the left side. A twenty-year-old woman could credibly strike with enough force to create Petty's mortal wounds. But as the town gossiped about what happened and as the prosecution and defense attorneys built their cases, plenty were asking whether it was believable that Alma had dumped the body into her trunk, stored it in her closet until the smell caused problems, moved it to the basement, dug a hole (albeit a shallow one) and buried the trunk all on her own. That's what she said. Many people doubted that's the way it happened. One newspaper headline bluntly said what plenty of townsfolks were thinking: "Mrs. Gatlin had help: The jury cannot be expected to believe she buried her father's body without the aid of someone."

Both Alma and her husband were arrested and held for the coroner's jury. Alma sat in the courtroom of the county's new municipal building as Reverend Pardue gave damning testimony about her confession to him. She looked steadily at him, relaxed and unfazed. During a break,

She Will Take Stand This Morning

Alma Petty during her trial in 1928. *Photo from Greensboro News & Record, February 18, 1928.*

Alma reportedly read the newspaper account of the case and "joked" with her attorneys. Her husband, though released from custody after the hearing established that he played no role and had no knowledge of the crime, was clearly "brokenhearted." Her attorneys assured reporters and anyone who'd listen that the case would fall apart and she would not be convicted.

TIME magazine noted that Southern newspapers covered Alma's trial in detail, though Northern papers chose to ignore it. When her case came to trial, Alma took the stand and offered a different version of events from what Reverend Pardue told. She described the night before the murder, when her father came home roaring drunk. He cursed and threatened the family throughout the hours after midnight, which was his pattern when drunk. The next morning, Alma said she was washing her neck at the kitchen sink when he came to the doorway and said, "You needn't be washing your damned neck. I'm going to cut it off—now!" He brandished a butcher knife. Alma's mother rushed into the tussle in the kitchen and struck him with the axe.

Smith Petty lay dead, but Alma's mother refused to call the police. She insisted on keeping the family's ugly secrets hidden, the way she always had.

In court, defense lawyers fought to keep Reverend Pardue from testifying, but the judge allowed the jury to hear his version. The state's attorney, in his

Rockingham County Courthouse in Wentworth stands on the right. The old county jail is on the left. *Courtesy of Indy beetle via Wikimedia Commons.*

closing argument, said, "They spend more time denouncing him than they do arguing that the defendant didn't do it."

According to the court coverage in the *Greensboro News & Record*, the trial was going well for the defense before the preacher took the stand for the prosecution. True, "the preacher had stood up well in his testimony, had met the defense's onslaughts with the irresistible might of meakness [*sic*]." However, Reverend Pardue faced sharp criticism for breaking the bonds of the confessional and voluntarily alerting police—in multiple visits—about the murder and Alma's role. "Mr. Pardue has been bitterly scorned by pulpit, press and public" for the part he played, starting long before Alma's trial.

In the aftermath of the controversial electrocution death of Ruth Snyder following her New York trial—photographed by an ambitious journalist who wore a camera strapped to his ankle to capture her death in the chamber—women's organizations in the Northeast rallied to Alma's cause. One group was focused on calling attention to the trial itself. Another was prepared to bring legendary attorney Clarence Darrow to North Carolina should she be convicted, to wage battle for the "nineteen-year-old girl wife" (though Alma was twenty-one at the time of the trial).

In the end, no outsiders needed to rally to save Alma. The jury acquitted her, and she walked from the courtroom with her husband.

At least one person had unwavering faith that Alma would be exonerated: Mrs. W.S. Timberlake (as married women were identified at the time), the county's court stenographer for many years. On March 28, 1928, she told reporter J.W. Cannon of the *Greensboro Daily News* that she seldom misjudged a case tried in her courtroom. "All during the trial, I kept saying to myself, 'Poor Alma, you don't belong in this courtroom. You didn't kill your father even though you told Mr. Pardue that you did. You were shielding someone else.'"

In June 1928, after the dust had settled, the *North Carolina Law Review* published an article exploring the legitimacy of Reverend Pardue voluntarily reporting Alma's confession to law enforcement. Because Alma was acquitted, the state's appellate court did not hear the issue in a formal legal appeal, so the questions remained unsettled: In confessing to a minister, was her confidence protected by law? If he breached her confidence, could his statement about her confession be admitted in court?

Trial judge Cameron McRae had held that the testimony could be admitted. The law review note pointed out that early Roman law did not allow the spiritual adviser to break the confidence; as an agent of God, the message passed straight to Him and "the priest could lawfully and rightfully swear that he knew nothing of it." After that time, religious confessional cases continued to be rare and the holdings unpredictable—some said yay, some said nay. About half the states had passed laws protecting the penitent privilege; notably, the only Southern states were Arkansas and Kentucky. Some jurists contended that "ministers should be just as free to yield to their consciences and notify the police as criminals are to yield to theirs and confess to ministers," but many state statutes supported priest-penitent confidentiality, just as they protect lawyer-client and doctor-patient confidentiality.

Phil Link, who was less than a decade younger than Alma Petty Gatlin, waited until her death to publish the book he was researching. In 1991, he started digging through the newspaper clippings and state archives. In 1992, he contacted Alma in Columbia, where she ran Gatlin's Rest Homes after her husband's death in 1952. The couple had three children, and she was a member of the Eau Claire Baptist Church, having made her profession of faith when she was twenty-six years old. Alma died in 2001 at the age of ninety-five, known as a gracious, God-fearing woman who'd raised her children, taken care of aged folks and lived a quiet life. In 2002, Phil published the story that had drawn thousands of curious court-watchers to the little county seat of Wentworth for Alma's trial.

TED KIMBLE

Those who grow up in the small-town South are bound to one another by strong ties, particularly family and faith, even when one or the other of those bonds might be strained by sin or straying.

In the mid-1990s, Pleasant Garden, south of Greensboro, with a population of four thousand, was one of those typical small Southern towns. Ted Kimble's father was a preacher at one of the town's churches. As a young man, Ted always had a line of girlfriends, but on May 7, 1994, he stood at the front of Monnett Road Baptist Church with his father, the officiant, and watched his wife-to-be walk down the aisle toward him. Those who knew Ted felt his wedding vows, Patricia's steadying influence and her obvious devotion were what he needed to finally settle down. To Patricia, Ted seemed devoted to making her happy; they both wanted children, and he was ambitious. She wanted so badly to make her marriage work that she struggled to lose weight to please him and welcomed him into the house she'd purchased on her own before they started dating.

The timing was perfect because Ted's mentor, Gary Lyle at Lyle's Building Material, was willing to sell him his building supply business if Ted demonstrated that he was ready to settle down. Gary Lyle knew Patricia was hardworking and good with her money, but he later said he never explicitly told Ted he wouldn't sell him the business if he wasn't married.

After their wedding, Ted took over the building supply, though he lacked the attention to detail that Gary had lavished on it. Despite Ted's business prospects and Patricia's job, paying the bills started to be a problem for the couple. They made plenty of money, but Ted liked toys—a boat, a motorcycle, a Magnum rifle. Patricia's careful budgeting cramped his lifestyle choices, but only a bit.

The happy story of the churchgoing young couple building their future together came to a tragic end only seventeen months after their May wedding. Just before 8:30 p.m. on October 9, 1995, fire trucks were called to the Kimbles' home on the Brandon Station Court cul-de-sac. Thick smoke filled the house, and responders spotted flames in a hallway near the bedroom.

After they extinguished that blaze and as large fans started venting some of the heavy smoke, one firefighter continued pulling a hose farther into the house to check the back rooms. Visibility was poor, and he suddenly fell through a four-foot-wide hole burned into the floor. He landed in the crawl space on top of smoldering debris. He soon discovered that the debris was more than remnants of insulation and flooring. The mound included Patricia Blakley Kimble, dead.

Examining the house later, after the smoke cleared and her body had been taken for autopsy, firefighters could see a burn path leading down the hall to the hole in the floor. That was enough to raise suspicion that this had been something more than a tragic house fire.

The autopsy confirmed their suspicions. Patricia died of a gunshot to the back of her head. The fire was started to obscure evidence and distract responders from discovering the murder.

Ted and other family members had alibis, and no one could figure out anyone with a motive for killing her. Guilford County sheriff's investigators considered whether she'd surprised a burglar and looked into a possible connection with burglaries in the neighborhood over the past two years. A man had been arrested for one of those break-ins. Detective Jim Church asked the convicted burglar to take a look at the insurance claim filed for a prior burglary at Patricia's house. "I didn't take half this stuff," he said. Ted had signed that padded insurance claim, which gave the detective another piece of the puzzle.

The more questions investigators asked, the more the picture of the perfect young couple began to chip and crumble. In an anonymous phone call to the Crimestoppers tip line in Greensboro, someone who knew Patricia said she confided that she was afraid her husband was going to kill her. Patricia's worries took shape when she learned Ted forged her signature on a life insurance policy; she had refused to sign the application when he presented it to her—a $100,000 policy that became $200,000 in case of accidental death.

The family was also surprised when Ted insisted on cremation; he said that's what Patricia wanted, but cremation wasn't something she'd ever talked about with her family.

Some knew that, before the couple married, Ted had been dating Patricia's cousin. He'd proposed to her more than once, the latest only weeks before he proposed to Patricia. Investigators added that interesting tidbit to their growing list of revelations. Less than two weeks after Patricia died, Ted started dating again. That news incensed a church member enough that she called the police.

Ted had always been a ladies' man, which wasn't a reason to suspect him of murder. When confronted about the forged life insurance policy, Ted

Marine training at Camp Lejeune near Jacksonville, North Carolina. *Courtesy of Lilibeth Serrano, Public Affairs Specialist, US Fish & Wildlife Service via Wikimedia Commons.*

Prayer Chapel at Liberty University in Lynchburg, Virginia. *Courtesy of PCHS-NJROTC via Wikimedia Commons.*

explained it away, saying he didn't want to nag Patricia to do something he knew was a good idea.

The investigation then turned to Ronnie Lee Jr., Ted's younger brother. At the time the shooting and arson occurred, Ted's brother had been on leave from the Marine Corps and was in Pleasant Garden helping out at Ted's business. Ronnie was stationed at Camp Lejeune near the coast in Jacksonville, North Carolina, so investigators made the two-hundred-mile drive to interview him on base. They found him a bit odd. Others had told them that his learning disabilities had made his childhood a challenge. His brother Ted was seen as the bright star in the family, the one Ronnie tended to follow. From their conversation with him, investigators knew he was the family member they could most likely persuade to talk. He seemed to care about Patricia, repeatedly asking in his initial interview, "Who would want to do this to Patricia?"

In a small town, people know one another. And they talk. In this case, developments provided plenty to talk about. The sheriff's office also had its regular caseload to investigate, including a rash of construction site thefts. Interestingly, the name that came up as they asked questions about the thefts was Michael Melton, one of Ted Kimble's employees at the building supply company.

Then an even odder lead came into the office. Jerry Falwell Jr., son of televangelist Jerry Falwell and an attorney at Liberty University, called to say he had information to share. Detectives drove the two hours to Lynchburg, Virginia, where they met the Wheelers, Mitch and Debra. Mitch had confided in attorney Falwell, who made the call so Mitch could tell the detectives what he knew.

Mitch was studying to be a minister at Liberty, but before that, he'd been stationed with Ronnie Jr. at Camp Lejeune. Ronnie was interested in Mitch's studies. That might be a post-military career option for him too, following in his own father's ministerial footsteps. Ronnie and his wife, Kimberly, came to visit the Wheelers and tour the campus. While there, Kimberly got a call that detectives had interviewed her parents again, with more questions about Patricia's death. Something was weighing heavily on Ronnie that weekend, and his religious conversations with Mitch often grew agitated. The evening after that phone call, he continued to fret about why Kimberly's parents were being questioned and finally said, "I did it, Mitch. I killed her. I killed Patricia. I shot her in the head, then set her body on fire."

The reason? "My brother paid me to do it." Confessing seemed to ease his tenseness. He told Mitch he didn't want anything to do with the money, that he'd donate it to Liberty University. Mitch discouraged that, said it was blood money.

Ronnie refused when Mitch urged him to go to the police. The next morning, after the Kimbles left without saying goodbye, Mitch sought advice from Jerry Falwell, who acted as intermediary and called Detective Church.

Meanwhile, in the investigation into the construction site thefts, suspect Mike Melton was more than willing to trade what he knew about Ted Kimble and Patricia's murder. Ted had planned the thefts and threatened to kill the two men carrying them out if they talked. Ted assured them he'd gotten away with murder for over a year, and he could do it again. He even showed them books he had about how to get away with murder.

The investigation also uncovered that Ted had a history of insurance frauds.

Ted and Patricia had been married for seventeen months. The investigation leading to the arrest of Ted and Ronnie took eighteen months. On April 1, 1997, the carefully planned and closely timed arrests took place. Ted was pulled over on Woody Mill Road as he drove to work, while Ronnie was taken into custody by military police at Camp Lejeune.

Ronnie was tried first, and in August 1998, he was found guilty of murder and arson. He initially faced the death penalty but was sentenced to life in prison without parole.

Ted closely watched what happened in Ronnie's six-week-long trial. Five months later, he decided to plead guilty, but just before he was to be sentenced, he tried to back out of the deal, saying he wanted to represent himself. The judge refused to allow a do-over and sentenced him to 107 years for second-degree murder. He was also convicted in the series of construction-site thefts he masterminded. The brothers remain incarcerated in separate North Carolina state prisons.

This story likely would not have drawn attention outside Pleasant Garden and the families and friends of those involved but for the work of Lynn Chandler-Willis. She went to school in Pleasant Garden before heading to Greensboro College and a corporate career, but she returned in 1996 to start the *Pleasant Garden Post*. As a journalist, she followed the arrests and trials of the two hometown brothers and later wrote a book-length account of the crime and the trials. Without Lynn's careful reporting, Patricia's death could've become another almost silent domestic tragedy. But a case where families, church members, law enforcement and friends are all so closely intertwined meant a tough balancing act in writing the book. In an interview with Nancy Bartholomew in 2000, Lynn explained why Patricia's devotion to Ted prompted her to tell this story:

> *It is important for us to help young people develop a strong sense of self. There is pressure on young people to have a girlfriend or boyfriend—our society fosters the idea that we are not a complete person without a mate. Consequently, people often choose mates that are not good for them. It happened to Patricia Kimble, but she didn't realize it until it was too late.*

6
FAMILY CONNECTIONS

THE LYERLYS AND THE DATA MINER

Sometimes a horrendous crime remains part of the local memory in hopes that those hearing it can learn from the mistakes and not repeat them. Often, though, the roots of some stories reach farther than the local storytellers know, part of a larger pattern that only becomes clear when someone digs deep and uncovers those other connections.

Bill James is an admirably gifted digger into facts and a weaver of stories. He's best known for his analysis of baseball statistics, made famous in the book and movie *Moneyball* about how the Oakland Athletics team began to apply the statistical analysis that James advocated. Neal Conan, an NPR interviewer, described James as "a guy working at that time as the night watchman at a pork and beans cannery in Lawrence, Kansas," when he started compiling his "Baseball Abstract." James later went on to work as a senior adviser for the Boston Red Sox.

James also brought those data-mining skills to his—surprising to some—interest in true crime. In his book *Popular Culture*, he analyzed news reports to develop a comprehensive list of explanations why some crime stories stay in the headlines and become part of popular culture and why some fade quietly from view. In a *New Yorker* interview, Evan Hughes called the book "something of a cult favorite among the crime-obsessed." James defended his crime obsession, saying, "I've always thought that these events are significant and serious events and people *should* pay attention to them. I've always thought interest in what I call popular-crime cases is a harbinger or a forerunner of some sort of effort to fix the justice system"—such as understanding how false confessions can occur or tracking the methodology of a serial killer. To do this, James used the same methodology he uses to track baseball statistics on bunts.

When Evan Hughes asked Bill James if he found studying crime "morally repugnant" or "exploitive," James replied: "What I find most offensive, honestly, is self-righteousness, the assumption of moral superiority. If people refuse to look at what really happens because 'well, you know, we are not the kind of people who take an interest in that kind of thing'… I find that more offensive than anything I have ever run across in a crime book."

James's research helped bring a broader perspective to a troubling 1906 North Carolina case and connected it with the story of a widely traveled serial killer he dubbed the Man from the Train.

The story of the Lyerly family, as students of North Carolina crime or Rowan County history will know, always focused on the killings, the lynch mob and the uncertainty of the guilt of those accused and hanged. Bill James's recounting of the murders of almost an entire family does nothing to lessen the horror of the murders or the aftermath but does provide a plausible solution to the mystery.

As James tells the story, it started late on July 13, 1906, with a man jumping from a slow-moving train at Barber Junction, located between Salisbury and Statesville. The mystery man headed for a white farmhouse maybe two hundred yards from where he got off the train. The house had sheltered members of the Lyerly family since early in the last century, through all the changes in fortune, failure and war that visited the South during those decades.

As usually told, the story starts with the four Lyerly daughters appearing in the dark morning hours of July 14 at the house of their neighbors, the Cooks. The older girls were carrying their badly burned and mortally injured youngest sister and telling of a horrific scene at their house.

Addie Lyerly had wakened about midnight struggling to breathe. She suffered from asthma, and the smell of smoke downstairs left her choking for air. Her parents and younger brother and sister slept downstairs, while she and her two other sisters—older and younger than she was—slept upstairs in the family's rambling wood-frame farmhouse. She explored the dark downstairs and found her father, Isaac, and mother, Augusta—Isaac's second wife—dead in their bedroom. The two younger children—nine-year-old John and six-year-old Alice—slept in the two separate beds with their parents.

Isaac's head had been bashed with the flat edge of an axe. The bed where he slept with his youngest son, John, was on fire, though nothing else in the room was burning. His wife was partially off her bed and covered with a pillow. Later, they found she'd been struck with both sides of the axe. Young Alice was alive but in terrible pain from her injuries.

Addie pulled her father and brother off the bed and away from the flames and then roused her sisters upstairs. They put out the fire, hauled the kerosene-soaked bedding into the yard and then put out the fire the smoldering bedding sparked in the surrounding grass. With no running water inside the house, they used water stored in the kitchen, then pumped and carried the rest from the well outside.

Once they averted the fire danger, the sisters carefully gathered up Alice and walked the three-quarters of a mile to the Cooks' house. On the way, they crept past the tiny houses of some of the sharecroppers who worked their father's land. In the cabin closest to their house lived Jack Dillingham and his family, a man their father had recently had words with, as he had with another worker who lived nearby, Nease Gillespie. The girls bypassed those cabins to reach the Cooks' house, a couple they trusted to help them.

Alice survived into the following afternoon before she died, leaving the three oldest sisters to mourn their parents and two youngest siblings while speculation, anger and eventually violence swirled around them in the days following that unexplainable night.

The day little Alice died, the community began demanding justice. John Charles McNeill—known widely as the state's unofficial poet laureate—wrote: "This is a horrible story, but it is true so far as words can reproduce the scene, and its record should not be lost from the annals of crime." A century later, in his initial blog post about the Lyerly family, statistician Bill James included McNeill's call that this was a story that should not be lost.

A news reporter described buggies and horses and crowds of people gathering in the grove of trees in front of the Lyerlys' house, speculating about who'd killed them and planning how to address the crimes.

After the early morning alarm was raised, the closest sheriff was summoned by telegram from Forsyth County; he arrived about four o'clock that morning. Another telegram asked the governor to send bloodhounds. In a place and time where rural folks were used to taking care of matters without much outside assistance, some identified the likely culprits even before the sheriff rode into town.

By the morning of July 14, neighboring sharecroppers Jack Dillingham—who'd had words with Isaac Lyerly the week before about something—and Nease Gillespie, whom Bill James described as "not quite likeable enough to be called a 'character'—had been arrested. They also arrested the wives of Dillingham and Gillespie, along with Gillespie's son and two other men. The job of the sheriff and some other sensible men in the community turned to averting a lynching. They moved the prisoners about forty miles away to the jail in Charlotte for safekeeping. The following month, when things seemed under control, they moved them back to Salisbury for a grand jury hearing.

Over the following decades, the story told locally focused on the tragedy that took place at the county seat in Salisbury, where deputies sat with rifles across their knees as hundreds gathered in the streets. The railroad ran through Salisbury. Reporters traveled by rail to carry news to Charlotte as protestors and agitators arrived by rail from surrounding areas. More outsiders flooded into town, and the sheriff asked that the local militia, the Rowan Rifles, be mobilized and sent to the courthouse.

Twenty or thirty years earlier, in the late 1800s, hanging had been the businesslike way to punish crime in a community. Organized law enforcement was often too far away and too few to handle local issues. Often, a judicial hanging would be carried out after a formal trial. Other times, it might result

Union train depot in Salisbury. *Courtesy State Archives of North Carolina via Flickr.*

from swift and summary judgment after a coroner's jury hearing rather than waiting for a formal trial. Whites as well as Blacks were thusly punished in those days before 1880. Following a particularly heinous crime, especially one involving children, large mobs and threats of lynching weren't uncommon outside courthouses. In upstate South Carolina in 1950, a mob of four thousand gathered outside the Oconee County Courthouse after a white man was arrested for kidnapping, assaulting and murdering two little girls; the sheriff successfully subdued the crowd, and the killer was transported to Georgia and later tried and executed in North Carolina's electric chair for his multi-state crime. (See *True Crime Stories of Western North Carolina*, The History Press.)

But in Salisbury, the anger over the Lyerly murders couldn't or wouldn't be diverted—and that tragedy has been the focus of the story. Outside the courthouse in Salisbury, the crowds seeking to carry out mob justice became larger and, apparently, more ably led. The Rowan Rifles found themselves unable to control the growing crowds and the direct attack on the jail where the defendants were held. The governor sent militias from Charlotte, Greenville and Statesboro, but they arrived too late.

The mob who took over the jail "roughed up" the two women and the children held inside but left them locked in their cells. The vigilantes held a trial of sorts and acquitted two of the men, but they locked them in cells to protect them from the crowds outside. They found guilty those first suspected: Nease Gillespie; his son John, age fifteen; and Jack Dillingham. They paraded them from the jail about a mile through Salisbury to a large old oak tree in Worth Park. Despite attempts to force them to confess, all three maintained their innocence. All three were hanged before lunch on August 6, 1906.

More than one hundred years later, blogger Scott Huler was following the path of John Lawson, an English explorer who left Charles Town, South Carolina, in 1700 and traveled through the Carolinas backcountry to the North Carolina coast. In his book, *A Delicious Country*, he wrote about his Salisbury stop in July 2015 and a chat with two men on a back porch.

As with much oral history, the locals' information had some holes: they named Seventeenth Street instead of Eleventh as the site of the lynching and five victims rather than three. Huler dutifully took a photo of the broken old tree they identified as the hanging tree, but later research raised doubts that it was really the tree at all. His conversation with the two men impressed him with how vivid and alive a history can be in the life of a community, more than a century later, despite the muddled details.

SALISBURY, N. C.   Rowan County Court House and Jail

Rowan County
courthouse
photographed
circa 1905–10.
*Courtesy of North
Carolina Collection
Photographic Archives.*

Even in 1906, plenty of people in Rowan County doubted that they'd punished the right men. Plenty of people recognized the atrocity of the hangings for what they were. And plenty of speculation circled about who actually killed four members of the Lyerly family and why.

Certain elements of the crime scene were noted that night and the next day: The attacks happened near midnight. Money was in view inside the house, available to a thief, but it wasn't taken, and there was no apparent motive. The blunt edge of the axe was used on most of the victims, and they were each hit in the head. A pillow was put over the mother's head. The fire was set after the murders. The victims were attacked while they slept. The house was in a rural farm area, an easy walk to the railroad tracks at a spot where a train would typically slow down. At the time, these facts were noted, but their importance in connecting them to a long chain of other murders was not clear until decades had passed.

Data expert and baseball writer Bill James is fascinated by what we can learn about the past by gathering and studying key data. He first became fascinated with the murders of eight members of the Moore family—six of them children—in Villisca, Iowa, on June 9, 1912. Today, among true crime historians, the name Villisca is synonymous with this brutal killing, and the Villisca Ax Murder House can currently be rented for tours and overnight stays.

With research assistance from his daughter, Rachel McCarthy James, Bill James began digging through news reports looking for other family murders that occurred along railroad tracks early in the twentieth century. Their search parameters listed thirty-three elements they had linked to a serial killer who moved north and south along eastern railway lines until about 1908 and then started moving east to west after 1909. James calculated that the odds of finding a "random match" for this list of elements in another family killing would be billions to one. A scene with one or more of the elements isn't unlikely. But all thirty-three elements—or most of them? "The odds against there being a *random cluster* of such events, with no one criminal causing the cluster, would be astronomical," wrote James.

The Lyerly murder scene had several of the elements they had found in other family murders, what they believed were the defining characteristics of a prolific serial killer. First in his blog, *Bill James Online*, and later in a 2017 book, father and daughter outline the cases that fit the key crime-scene elements. They dismiss famous murders that happened near railroad tracks but don't fit the parameters, and they name the man most likely responsible for over one hundred deaths spread over more than a decade. The Lyerly murders fit solidly within the parameters of the serial killer's victims, even though in this case, the man didn't search upstairs and therefore left the sisters alive, and he didn't lock up the house and jam the door so it couldn't open, as the killer usually did.

James theorizes that the man heard the train coming in the distance and knew he had only minutes to leap onboard and escape without time to finish his ritual behavior. He likely wasn't in the habit of buying tickets but instead just jumped on the first slow-moving train that came along and carried him away from the scene.

By tracing the path of killings that met the thirty-three elements in the Man from the Train murders and by simultaneously tracing the path of a man who likely murdered his first victim in 1898 in Massachusetts, they identified Paul Mueller as the killer. He likely arrived at Rowan County's Barber Junction after killing a Florida family. Afterward, without all his customary rituals fulfilled at the Lyerlys, he took an unexplained eighteen-month break before resuming operations in Georgia. The chain of murders ended in 1912 as mysteriously as they began, after upending hundreds of lives and communities just as the crimes had in Salisbury.

James lists other crimes where police and the public simply couldn't or wouldn't believe, at first, that multiple murders were connected: Jack the Ripper; the BTK killer in Wichita, Kansas; and others. One tenet of crime investigation is that the victims usually know their killer. If that's not true, James writes, "Well, you know, otherwise we would have to believe the family was a victim of a roving monster, and we can't believe *that*." The reluctance to believe in monsters is strong, even when a string of murders happens in a single city. Spread the murders over hundreds of miles and dozens of locales, without modern forensics and communications, and making a connection becomes insurmountably difficult.

Nease Gillespie, John Gillespie and Jack Dillingham were also victims of the man from the train. In all, fifteen people were imprisoned, legally executed or illegally lynched for his crimes. In 1906, no one had the means to track the monster who came and went by rail. They could only look closer to home—even when that's not where the monster lived.

THE LAWSON FAMILY CHRISTMAS TRAGEDY

In Germanton, just north of Winston-Salem, Christmas Day 1929 saw a family tragedy that made newspaper headlines across the country and remains memorialized in books, documentaries, podcasts, books, articles and even in a local museum.

The terms *family annihilator* or *familicide* hadn't been coined in 1929, but when Charlie Lawson took two long guns and killed his wife, six of his seven children and finally himself, he helped establish the definition of a man who annihilates his family.

The *Twin City Sentinel*, one of Winston-Salem's newspapers, summed up the crime in its headlines the day after the murders: "Suicide Slays Seven; Stokes County Farmer Kills Wife and Six of Children; Charlie B. Lawson Wipes Out Every Member of Family Except Son Away on Visit; Two Guns Used; Five Bodies in House; Two in Barn; Slayer in Woods; All to Be Buried in One Grave Friday."

Charlie Lawson was a tobacco farmer and member of the Germanton Council, Junior Order United American Mechanics. Members of that fraternal organization served as pallbearers and organized the family's graveside service.

Under the newspaper headline was a charming recent family portrait. The only survivor, son Arthur, age sixteen, stands in the left of the photo next to his older sister Marie, age seventeen. He is dressed in a three-piece suit and tie, slender and taller than his father, who stands on the other side of Marie. Beside Charlie, age forty-two, stands his wife, identified in the news caption as Mrs. Lawson, age thirty-eight. She is holding their one-year-old baby, Mary Lou. On the front row sit the younger children—two boys and two girls, ranging in age from two and a half to thirteen. In hindsight, the trip into town and the money spent on clothes and on the photographer were unusual expenditures for a large farming family usually strapped for cash. Given what happened, why was this photo important to Charlie Lawson?

On Christmas Day, Charlie's brother Elisha was out doing some hunting with a group of men when he stopped by Charlie's house. No one answered his knock, so he peeked through the window, where he saw Mrs. Lawson and three children—Marie and the two youngest boys, James William, age four, and Raymond, two and a half—lying on the floor.

The sheriff and coroner soon answered his call for help. No one dared touch the bodies until the officers arrived. After a search, the two youngest girls—Maybelle, age seven, and Carrie, age thirteen—were found in the tobacco barn. They had stones under their heads, as if resting on pillows. Blood evidence in the road indicated they'd been running for the barn when they were shot in the back and carried into the barn. Their mother was apparently killed first, as she held the baby. The victims were shot or bludgeoned with either the rifle or shotgun. The killer was deliberate and determined.

A portrait of the Lawson family in 1929. *Courtesy of North Carolina Department of Natural and Cultural Resources.*

Those at the scene that day recounted the awful juxtaposition of the children's Christmas toys and dolls with the horror of their deaths. "The children left their playthings as if they had been summoned to a meal, and the toys that they had enjoyed only a few hours were left as if awaiting their return. Close by were the carefully placed bodies."

They later learned that Charlie had sent his oldest son, Arthur, on an errand that morning. Why he was the only family member spared was never explained.

Charlie Lawson was missing from the scene. Thinking he might be holed up in the attic, a local doctor climbed upstairs to check. No one there. The men headed to the tobacco barn and followed a track about three hundred yards into the pine woods. Charlie Lawson had apparently put the shotgun to his chest and fired. The shotgun and a rifle lay beside him, along with a note: "Nobody to blame but—." He never finished what he had to say.

The initial theory was that a head injury Charlie suffered a year before caused him to suddenly go insane. Dr. B.J. Helsabeck, the Lawson family's physician, who also served as coroner for Stokes County, removed the brain looking for a physical explanation but found no external evidence of damage.

The Christmas holiday had brought one gift to help explain the sad scene. Sheriff John Taylor's brother, Dr. Spotswood Taylor, was in town visiting family for the holidays. The surgeon from Johns Hopkins Hospital in Baltimore assisted Dr. Helsabeck in the autopsies. The two physicians closely examined Charlie's body, and Dr. Taylor carried the brain with him to Baltimore for further study "in an effort to discover what type of insanity was responsible for Lawson's action."

Dr. Helsabeck later told the *Twin City Sentinel* that they'd found "a low-grade degenerative process in the middle of the brain." While they didn't find any evidence of an external injury to his brain, this "unusual spot in the center…is not filled out in proportion to the rest." In caring for Charlie Lawson as his family physician, the doctor said, "I have noted during the past twelve months that Lawson was acting queerly. He had been coming to me with complaints of severe headaches." The coroner's verdict determined that Charlie had killed his family in a "fit of insanity." Could modern medical technology have provided a clearer explanation? Could it have prevented what happened on Christmas Day?

After laying his daughters' heads on stone pillows in the barn and crossing their arms over their chests, Charlie apparently returned to the house and laid out the others with their arms crossed. According to the *Twin Cities Sentinel*, "The Coroner said it was possible that with this act of tenderness a semblance of reason returned to the insane farmer, overwhelming him and causing him to rush from the house and slay himself."

The reasons why a father (or mother) decides to wipe out an entire family have been examined in recent decades, but the answers are still not clear. Forensic psychiatrist Dr. Park Dietz was the first to use the term *family annihilator* for the rare phenomenon. The more common, current term is *familicide*. Most of these killers are male, and about half of them die by suicide.

Was Charlie Lawson overwhelmed with financial problems? Were his headaches and odd behavior signs of some organic process or mental illness? Healthcare professionals and law enforcement are often no better able today to recognize the signs than they were one hundred years ago. While rare, these tragedies still occur, often in families thought to be normal, happy ones.

In studying the murders of families living near train tracks, Bill James also identified the commonalities of family murders that differed from the serial killer train murders, the rare but typical or "unremarkable" family murders like the Lawsons':

> *Unremarkable family murders usually occur in daylight or in the early-evening hours (because they usually occur in the context of a heated family dispute). Unremarkable family murders almost always are committed by a family member or a person close to the family such as a rejected suitor, a servant, or an overfriendly neighbor, often followed by the culprit's suicide. Often that person has a history of mental illness, alcoholism, or drug abuse, although in some cases the crime is committed due to greed.*

Sadly, the Lawson family murders fit this "unremarkable" template.

Five thousand people thronged to attend the family's funeral. The *Winston-Salem Journal*'s headline said that "friends and morbid-minded file for hours past bodies." Judging from the website for the Lawson Family Murders Museum, crime tourism isn't a modern invention. After the murders, Charlie's brother Marion opened the family home to curious visitors for twenty-five cents a head.

The family was buried in a single grave in a small cemetery in Germanton. One of the funeral officiants from the Primitive Baptist Church had known Charlie Lawson for sixteen years. In his eulogy, he said, "God alone knows why this terrible deed was done."

Lawson family gravestone, commemorating eight members who died on December 25, 1929. *Courtesy of Berean Hunter via Wikimedia Commons.*

According to one account, eldest son Arthur Lawson later married and had children of his own. Sixteen years after the deaths of his parents and siblings, he died in a car accident at the age of thirty-two.

The abandoned farmhouse eventually collapsed in the 1970s. Local accounts say wood from the house was used to build a bridge on Payne Road.

The Lawson Family Murders Museum operates in the town of Madison, about twenty miles from Germanton, on the second floor of the Madison Dry Goods—the former location of the T.B. Knight Funeral Home, where the Lawson family members were prepared for burial. According to an article on the Strange Carolinas website, people in the community have presented proprietor Richard Miller with newspapers, photographs and other items to add to the collection. Admission is free.

THE NEWSOM/LYNCH SOUTHERN GOTHIC

On June 23, 1985, the fiery explosion of a Chevrolet Blazer in the middle of the afternoon in a leafy, quiet suburb of Greensboro attracted attention. A crowd of investigators from an array of state and federal agencies converged at the scene on Highway 150 in north Greensboro. And reporters—some who'd been following pieces of the case for over a year—began putting together a story that was hard to believe, even when it was meticulously laid out in lengthy news articles and in a book by legendary true crime journalist Jerry Bledsoe.

Preceding the car chase that ended with the explosion, Fritz Klenner, son of a prominent and controversial Reidsville doctor, had fired an Uzi submachine gun on police officers near the entrance to Guilford College, at the intersection of busy West Friendly Avenue and New Garden Road. Two officers were wounded at that scene.

An hour later, someone in the Blazer detonated a homemade bomb placed under the passenger seat. In the remains of the vehicle, officers found the bodies of Fritz Klenner, his first cousin—and lover—Susie Newsom Lynch and her two sons, ages nine and ten. The two boys had been poisoned with cyanide and shot at some point before the explosion. Susie Lynch was sitting on top of the bomb, and Klenner was driving. A newspaper photo showed a debris field with scattered car parts, human remains, an empty plastic milk crate and other detritus cordoned off with caution tape. Official vehicles parked along the roadside, and men in suit coats and ties studied the ground, talking to each other, trying to understand what had happened.

The four deaths in the Blazer were the last in a series of nine violent deaths spread over almost a year within the extended Newsom and Klenner families. The first murders occurred in July 1984, with the deaths of sixty-eight-year-old Delores Lynch and her daughter Janie Lynch in their home in Prospect, Kentucky. At the time of the explosion, though, no one could have linked those deaths with the chain of events that would end in that Chevy Blazer.

Any good Southern gothic requires certain elements: tangled family ties, money and important social connections, tragedy, violence, at least some measure of mental instability and, at the extreme, incest. This case had it all. Weaving the various elements into a cohesive—though inconceivable—story took the dedicated work of four law enforcement agencies in two states and the dogged work of journalists.

The histories of the Newsom, Klenner, Sharp and Lynch families make a good starting point. The three Sharp sisters provided the connections. Florence Sharp married Bob Newsom Jr., while Annie Sharp married Dr. Frederick Klenner. Susie Sharp became the first woman to serve as chief justice of North Carolina's Supreme Court—and likely the first elected (rather than chosen by the other members of the court) female state chief justice in the nation. The three sisters were social stalwarts in their communities.

From his medical practice in Reidsville, Annie's husband, Dr. Klenner, was well-known in medical circles for his journal articles and his advocacy for massive doses of vitamin C to combat polio, multiple sclerosis and viruses. Some regarded the Duke Medical School alum as a talented healer; others called him a quack. He was also known as a staunch patriot, a hater of communism, a racist and a controlling, demanding father to his son, Fritz, who lived in his father's shadow. Dr. Klenner's patients loved him, and the family was prosperous.

Florence Sharp Newsom and her husband, Bob, settled in Winston-Salem, where Bob worked for R.J. Reynolds. They had one daughter, Susie. From her childhood years, her sense of entitlement and her temper tantrums were common knowledge.

Susie attended Wake Forest, where she had an active social life and met basketball player Tom Lynch, son of a wealthy family from outside Louisville, Kentucky. Tom's mother thought Susie a poor match for her son from the beginning, and her predictions started coming true on June 6, 1970, the day of their wedding.

The couple moved to Lexington for Tom to attend dental school, while Susie worked in an office. Susie, though, refused to visit her mother-in-law, Delores, who lived a little over an hour away. After graduation, Tom joined the Navy Reserve, and the couple moved to Beaufort, South Carolina, then to a practice in Albuquerque, New Mexico. Their two sons, John and Jim, were born, but Susie limited contact with their grandmother Delores. Tensions in the family increased. Susie volubly hated Albuquerque, its lack of style and culture. She told anyone within earshot about her wealthy, influential family in genteel North Carolina.

In 1979, she took her sons and left Albuquerque for Greensboro; then she moved with the boys to China, where she taught for a few months. No matter where she was or who was catering to her whims, nothing seemed to suit her. Soon, Tom and Susie were waging a custody battle between New Mexico and North Carolina.

Susie's cousin Fritz Klenner, five years younger than she was, had attended Ole Miss in Oxford, but he didn't graduate. Instead, he lied to his father about enemies who prevented him from getting a diploma. Then he lied about enrolling in Duke University's medical school and told convincing stories about how his professors regarded him as a genius. Fritz reported to his father on his quick promotion to a position doing important research and soon began wearing a white lab coat, working part-time in his father's office in Reidsville and doctoring on his friends with pills and plenty of vitamin C.

Dr. Fred Klenner, the child of German immigrants, became interested in orthomolecular medicine, an alternative medicine that used nutriments natural to the body to rebuild and strengthen the immune system. He'd met nursing student Annie Hill Sharp while they were both enrolled at Duke Medical School. He moved to her hometown of Reidsville and set up his office on the floor above Dailey's Drug Store on Gilmer Street. According to journalist Jerry Bledsoe, he had a reputation as a caring physician, making house calls and treating those who couldn't afford to pay him. World War II ignited suspicions about Dr. Klenner's possible Nazi sympathies, but he continued his research, published papers, cared for his patients and was even

South Scales Street in downtown Reidsville. *Courtesy of Indy beetle via Wikimedia Commons.*

recognized by others who also touted the benefits of vitamin C, including Nobel Prize–winner Dr. Linus Pauling. Klenner held some odd views, but as his nephew Robert Newsom III described him, "Ol 'Doc Klenner may have been a bit weird, but he was the one great eccentric without whom no large Southern family can function."

Dr. Fred was immensely proud of his bright, handsome, winsome son, but he could also hold a high bar for accomplishment. What Fritz failed to accomplish in reality, he concocted in intricately woven and persuasively told tales.

After Susie returned home with her sons in 1980, her mother insisted she visit her uncle Dr. Klenner because the stress of the separation and custody issues were affecting her health. Susie, in Winston-Salem, and her younger cousin Fritz, in Reidsville, hadn't lived near enough to each other to grow close as children. After Susie ran into her cousin Fritz during a visit to his father's office, the two started spending time together.

When her divorce became final in December 1982, she continued to limit Tom's access to his sons. Fritz, though, was spending more and more time with the two young boys and eventually moved into Susie's apartment. At that point, Fritz's wild, self-invented life began to coalesce with what some outsiders later described as Susie's fantasy princess world of entitlement. Her brother Robert III said that didn't accurately portray her. What some saw as imperiousness came from her sense of not belonging and, in response, "turning her sense of isolation into a feeling of specialness and privilege."

Fritz told anyone who'd listen tales about his heroics as a Green Beret in Vietnam and about his work as a CIA operative assigned to dangerous missions. For Susie, Fritz set himself up as her knight in shining armor and wove conspiracies about Tom's plans to kidnap her sons and how he would protect them. He recorded phone calls from Tom, threw away presents from Tom and from his mother, Delores, and insisted that their increasingly rare visits be closely monitored. As time passed, his wild tales of international intrigue and of Tom's perfidy mushroomed.

Concerned about the influence Fritz and Susie were having on his sons and how little time he got to spend with them, Tom Lynch, with financial support from his mother, filed a lawsuit seeking increased visitation. That action set off an unimaginable deadly chain of events—unimaginable, except that it really happened.

On July 24, 1984, Delores and Tom's sister Janie were found dead in Delores's Prospect, Kentucky home. Both had been shot in the back with an assault rifle. After the first shot to her back, Janie had the fortitude to run toward the phone and an alarm button in a bedroom before she was fatally shot in the neck.

Kentucky investigators contacted Tom Lynch in New Mexico as they tried to figure out who would execute his sister and his mother. At first, the scene was hard to decipher, but investigators' suspicions began to focus once they learned of the acrimonious custody battle. They had little physical evidence, though. Susie told them with certainty that the Lynches had been killed by Colombian drug kingpins and the Las Vegas mob, prompted by Tom Lynch through his connections. Fritz had given her that information.

Ten months later, on May 19, 1985, the Sharp sisters' mother, Hattie, age eighty-four, was found dead of multiple stab wounds, with her throat slit and a gunshot to the head. Her son Bob Newsom Jr. and his wife, Florence—Susie's mom and dad and Fritz's aunt and uncle—had both been shot to death. They were all at Hattie's home on Valley Road in Winston-Salem. The Newsoms and Tom Lynch had recently renewed contact with each other after the Newsoms reached out with condolences over the murders of Tom's mother and sister. Bob Newsom had agreed to testify on Tom's

Summerfield Town Hall. *Courtesy of Indy beetle via Wikimedia Commons.*

behalf and against his daughter Susie in the custody hearing scheduled for the following week. Investigators believed the timing was no coincidence.

Two weeks later, the Chevy Blazer would explode in Summerfield, north of Greensboro, surrounded by Forsyth County Sheriff's deputies, detectives from the Kentucky State Police, a detective and uniformed officer from the Greensboro Police Department and agents from the State Bureau of Investigation.

In fitting together the links between the widespread crime scenes, investigators were forced to focus on Fritz Klenner. The more people they interviewed, the more peculiar the picture of his personality became. He loved to hunt—one of the pastimes he shared with his often-forbidding father. He possessed an alarming array of weapons—the extent of his collection not clear until after his death. According to the thirtieth anniversary retrospective article by the *Greensboro News & Record*, investigators found a lengthy list of weapons, ammunition, gold, silver and cash in the apartment he shared with Susie, at his mother's home and in the remains of the Blazer. Officials found multiple semiautomatic assault rifles, submachine guns, several shotguns and pistols, more than a case of dynamite with blasting caps and powder, ammunition, hand grenades, tear gas, gas masks, bulletproof vests, handcuffs and two remote-controlled mines.

Fritz created a life of ever-more embellished stories of his brilliance, his heroism (he reportedly saved his father from certain death on more than one incredible occasion) and his clandestine adventures. His stories grew to the point that some guys he hung out with nicknamed him Dr. Crazy. At times, he said he'd faced death—from cancer or other dreaded diseases—only to be miraculously cured. He also used his stories to charm women—and their young sons. He took their sons camping, talked about guns and knives and things that intrigue boys, including Susie's two sons.

Naturally, investigators became interested in Fritz Klenner's whereabouts at the time Susie's in-laws were killed in Kentucky. That weekend, Fritz had an alibi. He'd been camping with Ian Perkins, a student at Washington and Lee University who'd grown up knowing the Klenner family in Reidsville. Though Ian was eleven years younger than Fritz, the two had gotten better acquainted in 1984 and had a deepening friendship. Fritz visited Lexington, Virginia, and Ian gave him a tour around his college campus. He shared with Fritz his dream of following his great-uncle into a career in government intelligence work with the CIA. Fritz told Ian about his work with the CIA, that he'd been recruited while he attended a private high school in Atlanta and that he'd faced death on some of his covert operations. He told tales of dealing with smugglers stealing U.S. military weapons and exchanging them for drugs in South America, about the drug dealers' Russian KGB connections and about killings he was contracted to carry out for the government.

Ian later explained to investigators that Fritz needed someone he could trust to accompany him on one of these secret kill missions. Ian agreed. This was a dream come true for a twenty-one-year-old who longed to be a spy. Finally, the mission was set for May in Winston-Salem: kill a drug dealer. Fritz paid Ian $300 to drive Fritz's Blazer from Lexington to Winston-Salem. Ian detailed the route they took, down Interstate 81 to Interstate 77, exiting at Mount Airy and ending at Reynolda Road near Old Town. Ian dropped Fritz off, and he disappeared into the trees carrying a briefcase with two pistols and plenty of ammunition.

Ian drove down the road and got coffee at a fast-food restaurant while he waited for Fritz to finish his mission. Ian didn't know until later, but he'd left Fritz about half a mile from Hattie Newsom's house.

When two detectives came to Ian's off-campus apartment to ask him about the camping trip and Fritz's alibi, they first had to convince him that Fritz wasn't in the CIA and that he wasn't a doctor. Investigators, for their part, had trouble believing that Ian hadn't connected the dots between where he dropped off a heavily armed Fritz and where Hattie Newsom and her son Bob Newsom and daughter-in-law Florence had been killed. But Ian thought they'd died on the next day, not the Saturday he'd traveled to Reynolda Road with Fritz. Once they convinced Ian of Fritz's many lies, he gave them all the details he knew. Ian proved an important link in tying Fritz to the deaths of Susie's grandmother and parents.

Another key element came when police learned of a traffic stop as Fritz drove back to Lexington, with Ian following him in the Blazer. As he often did, Fritz was driving below the speed limit, which caught the officer's attention. That stop, only a few miles from where Ian dropped him off near Hattie's house, corroborated that Fritz was in the vicinity at the critical time.

In trying to understand the peculiar dynamic between Fritz Klenner and Susie Newsom, investigators, friends and family compared notes. Susie, some said, was spoiled by her parents. She'd grown accustomed to having her own way. Before she transferred to Wake Forest, Susie attended Queens College in Charlotte from 1964 to 1966. Later, Dr. Charles Hadley, one of her professors, was interviewed about his now-infamous student, who liked to stop by his office and chat about the British royals. Dr. Hadley's 2021 obituary described his office as "a library, classroom, lounge, museum, gallery, and community center all in one." Students often stopped by to visit. "One time, I came back to my office and she had rearranged all of the photographs on the wall of the (British) royal family," he told an Associated Press reporter in 1993. "When I told her she really should have asked for my permission, she became very angry. She shouted: 'They were not in the proper order!' I had never seen that look in her eye. She looked like she could have killed." She returned to his office that afternoon to apologize, but the memory of her tantrum remained vivid.

Fritz was well attuned to the needs of women and could create for Susie the ideal shining knight for her beleaguered princess. She often described him as "my protector." Whose idea was this crazy plot to kill everyone who got in the way of life as they envisioned it? Susie and her boys without interference from the Lynch family. The two of them with plenty of money to continue the lifestyle they'd grown up with. Fritz was clearly a tactician and agitator. How much did Susie know—or encourage? Did their fantasies feed off each other in an evil symbiosis where they were the only ones who mattered?

When Jerry Bledsoe's *Bitter Blood* was made into a television miniseries, part of Susie's past came full circle. Her former professor from Queens, Dr. Charles Hadley, had first met Susie's family members when her aunt, state supreme court chief justice Susie Sharp, received an honorary degree at Queens. Attending the ceremony with her parents, her grandmother Hattie and her cousin Fritz was Susie's first visit to Queens. Dr. Hadley had long experience coaching actors how to speak with a Southern accent—including Vivien Leigh for her role in *A Streetcar Named Desire*. Years later and unrelated to his time as Susie's professor, he was hired as dialect coach for Kelly McGillis, Harry Hamlin and Keith Carradine for the *Bitter Blood* miniseries about the Lynch/Klenner case.

Though the story has been carefully reconstructed, the truth, if it could ever be known or understood, died in that fiery blast on Highway 150. Tom Lynch is the only one left to mourn his family.

THE HALLMARK GANG

News of a home burglary often encourages caution among those living nearby—if they even hear about it. Before the advent of online neighborhood groups, news of a burglary might not spread far. Not interesting enough to report in the paper, certainly not on the evening television news. Most of the time, burglaries are isolated affairs. A crime of opportunity—a door left unlocked, maybe committed by someone who'd visited the house as a worker or one of the teenage children's friends, looking for something small and portable. The more ambitious housebreakers are often looking for something to turn into drug money.

The homes of wealthy people, the kind who might keep a home safe for cash or jewelry, who display expensive silver pieces or easily pawned high-end furs, silver, gold, jewelry or collectibles, are usually protected by security systems or even by a patrolling private security agency, so burglaries are rare.

But in the 1970s, a large multigenerational crime family of confederates, part of a larger gang from Philadelphia, brought a targeted kind of terror to exclusive neighborhoods in cities up and down the Eastern Seaboard. From Philadelphia's Main Line to Florida, the gang would travel, in a good night hitting several homes in the same neighborhood.

One of their happy hunting grounds proved to be central North Carolina, particularly Raleigh and Greensboro. Joseph Theodore Wigerman and Junior Kripplebauer often worked with Junior's wife, Marilynne D'Ulisse (called Mickie), and they led a gang that sent out teams of four or five in widening geographic bands, ranging from Michigan and Missouri to Oklahoma, Texas and California. From 1968 to 1975, they hit about two hundred homes—sometimes returning to a house more than once. When they first drove into a town, they'd stop at a convenience store to pick up a city map and the newspaper real estate listings. Then they started their homework, looking for neighborhoods with homes selling for at least $500,000 (an amount close to $3 million today), for doctors' and executives' addresses and for Jewish synagogues and private golf clubs—the kinds of places located near where rich people would live. Mickie would find a Sears Roebuck for their essential supplies: chisels, crowbars, pliers, gloves, flashlights, footlockers, a sledgehammer. Sears' flashlights were best: bright and easy to hold in your mouth while rummaging for treasure.

Once they'd identified a likely neighborhood, they'd all dress in business attire so they would look like they belonged. They carried their tools in a briefcase to complete the camouflage. Mickie would dress in a dark skirted suit and a black wig. They'd drive the streets in Junior's Lincoln Town Car, studying the layout of different houses and looking for distinctive little red lights—the sign of a burglar alarm, the kind they knew exactly how to disarm.

A ring or two on the front door, followed by a purposeful knock—not loud enough to attract the attention of neighbors—would ensure no one was home. Then they'd move around to the back door, continuing to look for signs that anyone was in the house before they set to work. Meanwhile, Mickie D'Ulisse drove away and toured the neighborhood, on alert for police patrols and checking to see who was home, the layout of the driveways, how secluded the back entrances were.

At the house, Junior disabled the alarm system. Another guy would take a giant screwdriver and pop open the back door. Each member of the gang knew his role in the heist, and each played it well. One kept watch on the ground floor for police or family returning home. Junior and another guy scouted through the house to make sure it wasn't occupied, taking note of possible escape routes, all the while checking for anything of value. Junior always headed for the primary bedroom. They knew from experience that most people kept their valuables in the bedroom, wrongly assuming they'd be there to protect them if intruders came in the night.

If they found a safe, they drilled a hole and opened it. Most home safes weren't constructed to protect the contents from determined and experienced thieves. They moved quickly, loading their loot into the homeowner's luggage, packing the more fragile items so they wouldn't be scratched or broken.

Sometimes, if they were lucky, the driver reported back that the neighborhood offered more than one easy and lucrative target. The more they could hit in a sweep, the better for them. In quickly, then out of town. They loaded the loot in footlockers and shipped them air freight to Philadelphia. No reason to risk being stopped with a car trunk full of furs and jewelry.

Law enforcement—in particular, Raleigh detective D.C. Williams, Greensboro detective Larry Davis and Guilford County chief assistant district attorney Rick Greeson—began making links between these widespread burglaries executed with such similar tactics. They eventually partnered with investigators in New Jersey, Pennsylvania, the FBI and other jurisdictions to identify and build the case against the K&A Gang from Philadelphia. The gang was initially named for the intersection of Kensington and Allegheny Avenues in the historically Irish working-class neighborhood of Kensington, the site of the bar where the confederates met and made their plans. The gang later became known as the Northeast Philly Irish Mob, but in its heyday of daring burglaries in North Carolina, the K&A Gang was called the Hallmark Gang, the gang that stole nothing but the best, a play on the old Hallmark corporate slogan, "When you care enough to send the very best."

Kensington Avenue streetcar riot in 1910, later home of the Kensington and Allegheny (K&A) Gang in Philadelphia. *Courtesy of Bain News Service and Library of Congress.*

They knew where to find the very best. One of the burglaries, detailed by reporter Martha Woodall after the gang was captured, took place on March 8, 1975. Former Greensboro mayor Benjamin Cone—heir to the Cone textile fortune and a loyal University of North Carolina Tarheels fan—was at the Greensboro Coliseum cheering their ACC title win over rival North Carolina State. Oddly enough, according to author Allen M. Hornblum, the gang members shared a loyalty with both Duke and UNC–Chapel Hill basketball, often cheering their games at their favorite neighborhood bar back in Philadelphia's Kensington. After all, they felt a kinship with the region's wealthy corporate executives, lawyers, physicians and researchers, academics and heirs of industrial families who'd helped build the region's economy.

Benjamin Cone couldn't know that he would also participate in setting a record off the basketball court that night: the largest residential burglary in Greensboro's history.

That evening, the Hallmark Gang identified his Georgian Revival house in Irving Park as unoccupied and left with between $150,000 and $175,000 (close to $1 million today) in jewelry, silver and an ancient Roman coin fashioned into a necklace, one of only seven known to exist and the only one not held in the Louvre's collection in Paris. As was typical of their thefts, none of the items were ever recovered—including the rare Roman coin. Part of the gang's discipline was to keep nothing and move it quickly to fences in Philadelphia.

By 1976, thanks to the methodical work of the regional detectives and the multijurisdictional team of investigators, the gang's heyday came to an end when the first four of the thirteen participants were indicted. After he was locked up in the Guilford County jail, Wigerman first heard from a fellow inmate that they'd been given the Hallmark Gang moniker. They had no idea they were that famous in North Carolina. The gang also learned that in North Carolina, at the time, second-degree burglary was punishable by life in prison—the only state with such a tough penalty.

In 1980, Junior Kripplebauer and Mickie D'Ulisse—already divorced—pleaded guilty, with twelve to twenty years for him in addition to charges in other jurisdictions, and ten years for her.

In 1981, journalist Martha Woodall interviewed the gang members and wrote a detailed six-part series for the *Greensboro Record*. Over a thirty-year span, the gang stole $15 million worth of valuables (about $85 million today)—the equivalent of almost $3 million per year. True, they wouldn't have gotten the retail value of the goods by selling them to fences, but with a tax-free income, seems like they could have retired well. Unfortunately, the gang planned heists but not their retirement years. Ted Wigerman, one of the leaders out on parole when interviewed in 1982, was working at a landfill in North Carolina for a weekly paycheck of $140 (just over $1,700 a month today). He said, "I used to spend more on whiskey in one night than I now make in a week." He said he couldn't see going back to that life, even though it would be tempting if he continued making only $140. "Even then I don't think so. I had a long talk with myself."

When Martha Woodall asked Wigerman how he protected his own house, he said they left the phone off the hook (old-school advice now) and a television and a light on in the bedroom. He added, "There's really nothing you can do. If someone really wants to break in, they'll break in." But he warned against amateurs: "They don't know what they're doing and they panic." The heyday of the flashy house burglars was ending. Mickie, Junior's ex-wife, said, "And today, the junkies have ruined it."

SIDE TRIPS, CRIME BITS AND ODDITIES

DEVIL'S TRAMPING GROUND

A forty-foot circle bare of vegetation famous enough to have a stretch of state road named after it must be special indeed. About twenty-five miles east and slightly south from Asheboro and less than an hour from Greensboro is one of those oddities around which legend has grown. Cited in several books, articles and blog posts about spooky places to visit, the stories report weird sounds and how items placed in the circle are cast outside of it by the next morning. Those accounts don't exactly explain what's supposed to be so terrifying, though some 'possum and coon hunters reported being run off the property by a bear-sized "great black beast." The site's most consistent mystery is that nothing grows in the center of this large circle—some describe it as forty feet in diameter, though more recent reports measure it at about twenty mostly barren feet.

According to legend, its barrenness is blamed on the devil, who paces around and around plotting mischief and evil deeds. He's tramped there for many decades—accounts date back to the 1700s. The tales spread outside Chatham County thanks to John Harden's 1949 book, *The Devil's Tramping Ground*. According to the *Charlotte Observer*, that book sparked enough "lasting interest" that the state highway department installed signs pointing the way from nearby roads to the appropriately named Devil's Tramping Ground Road. What keeps the area clear of the trees and undergrowth found in the

Top: Sign directing visitors to the Devil's Tramping Ground off Glover's Church Road outside Siler City. *Courtesy DrStew82 via Wikimedia Commons.*

Bottom: The mysterious circle at the Devil's Tramping Ground, taken in 2017. *Courtesy of DrStew82 via Wikimedia Commons.*

At Devils Tramping Ground

Group of early visitors to the Devil's Tramping Ground. *Courtesy of digital collection of the Chatham County Historical Association.*

surrounding woods? The *Observer* listed the common speculation, ranging from its history as a Native American ceremonial site or a deer salt lick to an old cane sugar mill or a clay mixing plant. For a time, rumors of buried treasure brought seekers with shovels to the area. Paranormal investigators have visited the site, and some report seeing a mysterious fog moving among the trees.

Heather Leah dug into the story for Raleigh's WRAL News and reported that scientists from a regional lab and from the Soil Testing Division of the state's Department of Agriculture evaluated the soil and found it "sterile."

Rich Hayes, soil scientist from Chatham County, became involved in a more methodical study of the site around 2015. He looked for high salt or copper levels and tested inside the circle and around its boundaries to find variants from the surrounding soil. The data from his analysis didn't show any natural reason why plants wouldn't grow inside the circle, though the soil's makeup is different from the area around it. Maybe, he surmised, the bonfires regularly burned in the center of the circle have affected its fertility. He did find high pH levels and high readings of zinc. But the site isn't technically barren: reports dating back to the late 1800s describe the area with patches of wire grass, a hearty, clumpy grass that grows in a variety of landscapes— sunny or partial shade, in thickets or in swamps and alongside roadways. In summary, according to the North Carolina Extension Gardener's website, wire grass is "undemanding and low maintenance"—and apparently grows where the devil walks.

Maybe it's just that being isolated in dark, remote woods can feel scary. Maybe the sheer number of partiers who visit the circle to sit around a roaring fire explain the condition of the soil. After all, the devil may be the one tramping around and around the circle, but most of the others just come to party.

Please note: the circle is on private property and should not be visited without permission.

THE NO BODY CASE

For centuries, in common-law jurisdictions based on the English legal system, the rule was simple: no body, no murder. Plenty of killers still assume this is the rule, to their misfortune. According to Tad DiBiase, a former assistant U.S. attorney who tracks no-body homicide cases, over five hundred of these cases have been prosecuted in recent years. Surprisingly, the conviction rate is roughly 86 percent, compared with an overall murder conviction rate of only 70 percent.

In 1860, North Carolina was one of the first states to allow a murder prosecution without a body, but the original no-body prosecution was in 1660 and started with the disappearance of seventy-year-old William Harrison from Chipping Campden, England. Under intense—perhaps brutal—questioning, William's servant blamed his own brother and his mother for the murder. All three were promptly hanged. Months later, the presumed dead William Harrison miraculously reappeared with a stunning story of being kidnapped by Barbary pirates and sold into slavery in Turkey. He'd fortunately managed to escape, but not in time to save those convicted on the evidence of a bloody collar and an extorted witness.

England was justifiably horrified with the outcome of the bizarre tale, and no prosecution without a body took place in English courts for almost three hundred years. In North Carolina, though, the courts found grounds for allowing a prosecution exactly two hundred years after William Harrison disappeared.

In rural Rockingham County, north of Greensboro, Peggy Hilton, also known as Peggy Isly, disappeared on December 1, 1859. Evidence showed that neighboring farmer Robert Williams had been having "criminal intercourse" (sex without benefit of marriage) with Peggy for more than a year. Another young woman testified that he'd started courting her, and when she asked about Peggy, he told her he didn't know Peggy and certainly had no intention of courting her. But local gossip said otherwise.

In a 1995 interview, Bob Carter, a historical consultant for Rockingham Community College, described Williams as a prosperous farmer who owned 252 acres on Iron Works Road and served as an appointed justice, similar to a county commissioner today. A widower with three children, Williams was squiring around a "prominent lady of the area" but was also seeing Peggy Isly and, according to court testimony, at least one other young woman.

On Thursday night, Peggy walked out of her stepfather's house and vanished, carrying her best possessions bound up in her apron—a calico dress, two petticoats and a length of cloth.

Family and neighbors began searching for signs of her along Troublesome Creek, which ran on Williams's land. Among the ashes of a burned pile of logs, inside the hollow of a large stump and spread along the creek, they found bone fragments, part of a human skull, a cheekbone fragment, a few teeth, hair pins like those Peggy wore, a button, a hook-and-eye dress fastener and greasy residue.

Taken together, something dreadful had happened to someone on Robert Williams's property, and that someone was most likely Peggy. After the discovery, Williams and his workers dug up and turned the earth at the site before it could be further examined. He claimed he was merely preparing the ground for his garden, but in a farming region, plenty of people could testify about when, where and how a garden plot would be prepared.

The appellate court, in upholding Williams's conviction for Peggy's death, cited "celebrated Jeremy Bentham," an eighteenth-century English lawyer and philosopher, and allowed an accumulation of circumstantial and physical evidence to serve as proof of a crime. "Were it not so," said Bentham, "a murderer, to secure himself with impunity, would have no more to do but to consume, or decompose the body by fire, by lime, or by any other of the known chemical menstrua, or to sink it in an unfathomable part of the sea." The court upheld Williams's murder conviction, whose indictment stated was "moved and seduced by the instigation of the devil" to murder and destroy the body of Peggy Isly.

Starting in the 1980s, advances in forensic science and technology that allowed for sharing information among investigative agencies helped bring justice in a growing number of cases that previously were almost impossible to solve or prosecute.

Not until 1985 did North Carolina see another no body case, and the decision in *State v. Robert T. Williams* again made headlines. On July 18, 1983, real estate agent Dianne Gabriel left for an appointment to show a house near Lake Norman north of Charlotte. Two days later, her Buick Skylark was found abandoned in the parking lot of a local restaurant. Months later, some clothing, her handbag and car keys were found in the woods near the restaurant, but Dianne was never seen again. (See *Charlotte True Crime Stories* for more on this case.) In March 1985, Johnny Joseph Head was convicted of second-degree murder, based on fiber and circumstantial evidence. He served sixteen years of his sentence and was released in 2001, still insisting on his innocence.

No body prosecutions will always leave unanswered questions and uncertainty, which often result in lesser charges and shorter sentences because of the difficulty of establishing the planning or any of the aggravating or mitigating circumstances that might exist. Following the Head verdict, North Carolina has seen seven other no body prosecutions, scattered from 1988 to 2022, all made possible because of an old case and evidence found strewn on a creek bank in Rockingham County.

HENRY ALFORD AND HIS PLEA

On November 22, 1963, Nathaniel Young responded to a knock at the door by opening it a crack to see who stood outside. In Winston-Salem, his house was known as a party or liquor house. Nathaniel likely had only a split second to register who had come seeking admittance before the shotgun fired and killed him.

Earlier that evening, Henry Alford had brought his girlfriend to the party house, bought several drinks for the two of them and then spent his last dollar to rent a room so they could continue their party in private. The door to the room soon opened because Henry had no more money and his girlfriend wanted to stay and party with someone who did. Henry grabbed at her coat and was chased from the house by Nathaniel and another man.

A string of witnesses testified to seeing and hearing Henry Alford get the shotgun and shells, state he was "going to get Nathaniel Young," walk down the street and later admit that he'd killed Nathaniel Young with the gun.

Henry, though, officially claimed, "I ain't shot no man."

When Henry's own lawyer questioned the witnesses and all gave accounts contrary to Henry's version of what happened that night, the lawyer convinced Henry that the state's case was strong. The lawyer sat down with Henry, who had limited education, together with Henry's family and friends—including a police officer cousin—so they would understand what was at stake. He warned Henry that a jury would likely find him guilty of first-degree murder, given the mounting testimony, which would mean a mandatory life sentence or even the death penalty.

With Henry's written consent, his lawyer informed the solicitor and the judge that Henry was willing to plead guilty to second-degree murder, which had a maximum penalty of thirty years.

Accepting Henry's offer to plead guilty, the judge sentenced him to thirty years in prison. Not three months later, Henry filed a petition with North Carolina's supreme court, claiming he was forced into his plea by the "coercive threat of the death penalty." He said he'd been told he would be gassed if he didn't plead guilty, given "the circumstances that had got against me."

His petition to the North Carolina court was denied, so Henry continued to file appeals through the federal system. He contended that threatening a man with the death penalty to get him to plead guilty was unconstitutional and violated his Fifth Amendment right not to be influenced or coerced with either leniency or a higher penalty.

The issue became one of a man pleading guilty while maintaining his innocence. In North Carolina at the time, the difference in a life sentence and a thirty-year sentence would have been less than three years, given the parole options available. Henry was already fifty, so either sentence would be long for him. The case was argued twice before Chief Justice Burger's U.S. Supreme Court. The court ultimately held that judges could accept guilty pleas as long as the state presented substantial evidence of guilt and the defendant was fully informed of his rights in the situation. As now applied, the "best-interests plea" or Alford plea allows a guilty plea even though the defendant also maintains his innocence.

Courts do not have to accept plea deals, and three states—Indiana, Michigan and New Jersey—do not allow Alford pleas.

The U.S. Supreme Court's decision also contrasted an Alford plea with a nolo contendere or "no contest" plea, where the defendant admits neither guilt nor innocence but agrees to be punished as if he were guilty, and found no difference in practical application and upheld his conviction.

Why would a defendant professing innocence agree to be punished, either in an Alford or a nolo contendere plea? Obviously, it avoids the possibility of a harsher penalty at trial. But it also allows a defendant to avoid a trial and, at the same time, avoid having to say out loud that he committed a crime he'd rather not admit to in public, for whatever reason.

Plenty who follow court cases or watch television crime dramas have heard of Alford pleas—they make for great plot points. But few realize it all started on a night spent partying in a Winston-Salem liquor house in November 1963.

GOLD

In a 1799 tale that North Carolina schoolchildren learn, twelve-year-old Conrad Reed went fishing with his bow and arrow in Little Meadow Creek on his dad's Cabarrus County farm. As happens with twelve-year-old boys, his attention was diverted from fishing by an unusual yellow rock glinting in the water. He lugged the seventeen-pound rock home with him. Not able to identify it as anything other than interesting, his father, John, used it for a handy doorstop until 1802, when he took the rock to a Fayetteville jeweler. It was gold.

Maybe the silversmith didn't know what he was looking at—or maybe he did. He asked John Reed how much he wanted for it. "How about $3.50?"—about what a farm worker made in a week. The jeweler bought for himself one of the largest gold nuggets ever found east of the Rockies. (One larger twenty-eight-pound nugget was unearthed in the same creek in 1803.) The gold extracted from Conrad's nugget yielded a bar that sold for $3,600 (over $100,000 today).

To the relief of those who value fair play, John Reed heard about the sale and returned to the jeweler, who paid him a more equitable sum. John Reed then decided he would spend some time looking for yellow rocks as well as farming.

The rock that Conrad found started the first gold rush in the United States. Along a band running through North Carolina's Piedmont from Charlotte to Greensboro and into upstate South Carolina remained the center of gold-mining interests for thirty years. Then a larger strike in 1828, near Dahlonega, Georgia, shifted the search for gold to the area northeast of Atlanta in the Appalachian foothills. Twenty years later, in 1849, the California gold rush eclipsed the finds in the South, and the Civil War ended most of the gold mining activity in the Carolinas.

But for a time, the Reed discovery and its gold rush provided North Carolina with the first branch mint in the United States. Before the Charlotte Mint was opened in 1837, miners had to transport their gold to the mint

Top: Entrance to Reed Gold Mine, on the National Register of Historic Places. *Courtesy of Gus Jewell via Wikimedia Commons.*

Bottom: Photo of Mint Museum at the time of its opening as an art museum in 1938. *Photo courtesy of Whitsett Photography and the archives of the Mint Museum via Wikimedia Commons.*

in Philadelphia. The Charlotte Mint specialized in gold coins, issuing $5 million worth in the mid-1800s, almost $200 million today.

Confederate troops seized the southern mints in New Orleans, Dahlonega and Charlotte during the Civil War. After the war, federal troops occupied the Charlotte building during Reconstruction. The federal government refused to reopen the mint for operations, and the building was eventually targeted for demolition.

Mary Myers Danville, known as the "Mint's fairy godmother," spearheaded a movement in 1933 with the Charlotte Women's Club to save the condemned building. In 1936, the Mint Museum opened as the first art museum in the state.

The Reed Gold Mine is a North Carolina Historic Site and open for tours and panning for gold. See https://historicsites.nc.gov/all-sites/reed-gold-mine for information.

THE MILLION-DOLLAR BILL

At the Lexington Walmart on Lowe's Boulevard, a few days after Christmas in 2011, Michael Anthony Fuller loaded his shopping cart with a vacuum cleaner, a microwave and other purchases and made international headlines.

At the cash register, he handed the clerk a $1 million bill to pay for his $476 worth of purchases. Trouble was, $1 million bills don't exist. The U.S. government prints no denomination higher than $100, though they once printed (and would still honor) bills of $5,000 and $10,000—if they were legitimate.

Not that high-denomination bills don't exist elsewhere—the government of Zimbabwe, Africa, printed a $100 trillion bill in 2015. Thanks to hyperinflation in the country, the bill was worth about $0.50. The largest bill printed in the U.S. was $100,000 and used for only a couple of weeks at the end of 1934 and start of 1935 for transfers between Federal Reserve districts, not in public circulation.

As Leigh Goessl, reporter for the *Winston-Salem Journal*, noted, news outlets routinely cover cases of financial fraud involving stolen credit or debit cards or "the old standby of a bum check." Boldly offering a $1 million bill and insisting it was genuine, that was headline worthy. This wasn't, according to Goessl, the only fake $1 million bill in circulation at that time: someone put one in a Salvation Army Christmas kettle, and in Pennsylvania, a man tried unsuccessfully to use one to buy marijuana—a lot of marijuana, apparently.

Perhaps if Fuller had passed it off as a joke when challenged, he could have walked away, leaving his home-improvement goods behind. But he persisted, the police were called and he was arrested on felony charges for attempting to obtain property by false pretense and uttering a forged instrument.

Later, the charges were dropped by the Davidson County District Attorney's Office because of questions about the defendant's competency. He still faced charges for felony malicious conduct by a prisoner and misdemeanor assault on a government officer.

KÖRNER'S FOLLY

In 1878, the sign in front of the three-story, seven-level house at 413 South Main Street in Kernersville read "Körner's Folly." Some called it America's Strangest House.

Some likened the house Jule Körner (pronounced "Kerner") built to Sarah Winchester's much grander home in San Jose, California. Most histories of Sarah's rambling twenty-four-thousand-square-foot ornate Victorian "mystery" house, with its stained-glass windows, dead-end hallways and unexpected passages, say she built it to hide from the ghosts of those killed by the Winchester guns from which her family fortune derived.

But Jule Körner committed no crimes and wasn't running from ghosts or hiding secrets. He enjoyed operating his furniture and interior design business and wanted his house to be a living exhibition of his talents. He was the imaginative artist who created a national tobacco advertising campaign using the famous Bull Durham Bull. According

Example of an early Durham Bull advertisement in Collinsville, Illinois, one of six building signs known to remain. *Courtesy of Lyle Kruger via Wikimedia Commons.*

to Dan Sellers and Jeffrey Cochran in *Carolina Haints*, Jule understood that his anatomically correct bull had potential to, as we would say today, take the campaign viral. "Jule wrote to a local newspaper pretending to be a woman who was offended by the pictures. Then he wrote his own response to the letter, saying that without the genitals, 'you'd think it was merely a cow.'" Later ads added strategically placed banners so as not to offend.

Jule carried his creativity and whimsy into the design of his house. Every room offered a different experience, and he even designed whole house air-conditioning with tunnels under the floors and hidden vents for airflow. Construction was completed in 1880, while Jule was a bachelor. In 1886, he married Alice, the county sheriff's daughter, a woman who shared his whimsy and brought to the marriage her own artistic needlework skills. The lavish Victorian house, with its quirky rooms and intricate design, was ridiculed by some townsfolk, but dozens of the town's children attended Mrs. Körner's Juvenile Lyceum, where they could play musical instruments, make art or perform in plays for the community.

The house called Körner's Folly in Kernersville. *Courtesy of Upstateherd via Wikimedia Commons.*

An example of the creative work inside the whimsical Körner's Folly. *Courtesy of Amy Meredith via Flickr.*

Jule's bachelor billiards room was transformed into the elaborate Cupid's Park Theater, which is still used by community arts groups, and the second-floor ballroom still hosts events.

After Jule and Alice died, the house sat empty, and disuse took its toll. For a while, it served as a funeral parlor, and various other business plans were proposed. Finally, Körner's relatives bought the property, had it placed on the National Register of Historic Places and set about restoring it.

Naturally, in an odd house full of the personality of its original creators, rumors of ghosts flit about it. But the real draw is the amazing craftsmanship and the glimpse into a wildly creative mind. The museum house is open for tours, and its Christmas displays are especially popular. See https://kornersfolly.org for details.

REFERENCES

Welcome

Lane, Roger. *Murder in America: A History*. Columbus: Ohio State University Press, 1997.

1. The Poisoners

Nannie Doss, the Giggling Grandma

Crime Library. "Nannie Doss." Originally available on crimelibrary.com, article reprinted on murderpedia.com. https://murderpedia.org.

East, Bill. "Mrs. Doss, Husband Killer, Dies: Davidson Deaths Charged to Her." *Twin City Sentinel* (Winston-Salem, NC), June 3, 1965.

Goddard, Mary. "Nature Catches Up With Nannie Doss." *Daily Oklahoman*, June 3, 1965.

Manners, Terry. *Deadlier Than the Male*. London: Pan Books, 1995.

Rebecca Detter: Helpful Hitmen Are Hard to Find

Dorsey, Gary. "Arsenic Poisoning Case Going to Superior Court." *Sentinel* (Winston-Salem), January 13, 1978.

Jordan, Ronald. "Doctor Testifies Test Confirmed Poison in Detter." *Winston-Salem Journal*, September 22, 1978.

———. "Kernersville Woman Is Indicted in Arsenic Poisoning of Husband." *Winston-Salem Journal*, January 31, 1978, 7.

———. "Poisoning Death Charge Denied by Mrs. Detter." *Winston-Salem Journal*, September 23, 1978.

Olmstead, Rebecca. "Death—Or Life Term? Detter Jury Deciding." *Sentinel* (Winston-Salem), September 26, 1978.

———. "Hairdresser Says Woman Wanted Her Alibi Upheld." *Sentinel* (Winston-Salem), September 20, 1978, 13.

Patterson, Donald W. "Early Release Sought; Court Officials Protest." *Raleigh News & Record*, May 9, 1983.

Poindexter, Jesse. "Penalty Is Voided In Poisoning Case." *Winston-Salem Journal*, December 11, 1979.

Sentinel staff reports. "'Mrs. Detter Told Me to Keep Quiet.'" *Sentinel* (Winston-Salem), September 19, 1978.

State v. Detter, 260 S.E.2d 567 (N.C. 1979).

Blanche Taylor Moore, the Ministering Angel

Bowen, Russ. "Turning 90: North Carolina's Blanche Moore Is Oldest Woman on Death Row in US." *WBTW News 13* (Myrtle Beach), February 15, 2023. https://www.wbtw.com.

Leland, Elizabeth. "Arsenic Case Open For Him." *Charlotte Observer*, January 2, 1991.

Schutze, Jim. *Preacher's Girl: The Life and Crimes of Blanche Taylor Moore*. New York: William Morrow, 1993.

State v. Moore, 440 S.E.2d 797 (N.C. 1994).

Struck, Doug. "Pastor's Wife: Arsenic and Old Lace?" *Los Angeles Times*, August 22, 1989. https://www.latimes.com.

Wireback, Taft, and Justin Catanoso. "Blanche Taylor Moore Timeline." *Raleigh News & Record*, December 13, 2015.

Robert Coulthard and the Perfect Family

Associated Press. "Experts: Arsenic Poisoning Hard to Prove, Symptoms Hard to Detect." *Herald-Sun* (Durham, NC), February 11, 2001.
Grable, Mike. "Hospital, Seven Others, in Wrongful Death Suit." *Chronicle* (Duke University), September 15, 1989.
Keesler, William. "Man's Parole Eligibility Sparks Sad Memories." *Dispatch*, July 14, 2008.
Leland, Elizabeth. "High Point Arsenic Killing: All Clues Pointed to Husband." *Charlotte Observer*, December 1, 1988.
Lewis, Cynthia. "Monstrous Arrogance: Husbands Who Choose Murder Over Divorce." *Journal of Criminal Justice and Popular Culture* 15, no. 1 (2008). https://cynthialewis.net.
Stephens, Cinde. "Family Seeks Damages in Arsenic Death." *Greensboro News & Record*, August 11, 1991. https://www.greensboro.com.
Webb, Nancy. "High Point Man Gets Life Sentence for Poisoning Wife." *Charlotte Observer*, November 29, 1988.

For more on North Carolina's female poisoners, see cases in *Triangle True Crime Stories* and *True Crime Stories of Eastern North Carolina* (The History Press).

2. UNSOLVED

The Coffee Pot Case

Daily Charlotte Observer. "Case of Wholesale Poisoning." August 24, 1892.
Western Sentinel (Winston-Salem, NC). "A Whole Family Poisoned." August 25, 1892.
Zahrey, Luci, The Poison Lady. Personal correspondence, January 5, 2024.

The Party People

Bee (Danville, VA). "Mrs. Ballinger Was Murdered Jury Reports." January 18, 1929.
Colvin, Leonard. "Sex, Wild Parties and Two Unsolved Murders." *True Detective* no. 21 (2010): 43–45.

Greensboro Daily News. "Discover No Trail of Smith Murderer." September 8, 1929.

———. "Find Lifeless Body of Young Woman in Home; Pistol Near." January 16, 1929.

———. "Mystery of Girl's Death Is Thinning." January 18, 1929.

The Tragic Meeting of Wealth and Fame

Bradshaw, Jon. "The Notorious Libby Holman." *Vanity Fair*, March 1985. https://archive.vanityfair.com.

Clements, Caroline Sanders. "Who Killed the Reynolds Tobacco Heir? Revisiting One of Winston-Salem's Most Mysterious Deaths." *Garden and Gun*, November 13, 2023. https://gardenandgun.com.

Museum & Archives of Rockingham County. "This Month in Rockingham County History: August—Libby Holman Reynolds Turns Herself In at Rockingham County Courthouse." August 31, 2022. https://themarconline.org.

Schnakenberg, Heidi. *Kid Carolina: R.J. Reynolds Jr.* New York: Center Street, 2010.

3. The Lovelorn

A North Carolina Crime First

Lenoir News. "Gov. Craig Calls on Warren-Christy Attorneys to Present Case." March 3, 1916.

Robesonian. "Ida Bell Warren and Sam Christy Saved from Death in Electric Chair." March 23, 1916.

Twin-City Daily Sentinel (Winston-Salem, NC). "Mrs. Ida Ball [*sic*] Warren and Samuel P. Christy Taken to State Prison." March 16, 1916.

Winston's Wronged Lover

Brownlee, Fam. "Swinging into Eternity…Poor Ellen Smith." *North Carolina Collection* blog, Forsyth County Central Library, March 25, 2015. https://northcarolinaroom.wordpress.com.

Twin-City Daily Sentinel (Winston-Salem, NC). "A Sheriff and an Editor." August 19, 1892.

Union Republican (Winston-Salem, NC). "A Brutal Murder." July 28, 1892.

Western Sentinel (Winston-Salem, NC). "He Gave Himself Away. DeGraff Tells Why He Went to the Scene of the Murder." August 17, 1893.

———. "He Killed Ellen: DeGraff Makes a Confession on the Scaffold." February 8, 1894.

The Personal Ad Tragedy

Adams, Robin. "Bachelor Casts Bait, Is Surprised When He Gets Caught." *Greensboro News & Record*, January 4, 1988.

———. "Murder Weapon Search Begins: Divers Scour River for Gun Used to Kill Reidsville Man." *Greensboro News & Record*, June 25, 1988.

———. "Two Plead Guilty in Shooting Death of Reidsville Man." *Greensboro News & Record*, July 29, 1988.

Heller, Janice. "No Clues Yet in Reidsville Man's Death: Victim's Relationship with Woman Went Sour." *Greensboro News & Record*, April 26, 1988.

———. "Woman Jailed in Killing of Man She Met with Ad." *Greensboro News & Record*, June 24, 1988.

4. BLACK WIDOWS—AND A WIDOWER

Barbara Stager

Bledsoe, Jerry. *Before He Wakes: A True Story of Money, Marriage, Sex and Murder*. New York: Dutton, 1994.

Blythe, Anne. "Haunted, She Seeks Justice for a Stranger." *News & Observer* (Raleigh, NC), April 20, 2009. https://www.newsobserver.com.

———. "She's Serving a Life Sentence for Killing Her Husband. But She Goes Out to Lunch?" *News & Observer* (Raleigh, NC), October 31, 2018. https://www.newsobserver.com.

North Carolina v. Stager, 406 S.E.2d 876 (1991).

Betty Lou Beets

Beets v. Texas, 767 S.W.2d 711 (1987).

Pence, Irene. *Buried Memories: The Chilling True Story of Betty Lou Beets, the Texas Black Widow.* New York: Pinnacle, 2001.

Sealy, Geraldine. "'Black Widow' Executed: Great-Grandmother Is 4th Female Inmate to Die in U.S. Since 1976." APBNews/AP, February 24, 2000.

UPI Archives. "A Twice-Widowed Woman and Her Daughter Have Been Charged." UPI, June 9, 1985. https://www.upi.com.

Tim Boczkowski

"All Wet." *Forensic Files*, season 7, episode 42, first aired June 4, 2004.

Commonwealth of Pennsylvania v. Boczkowski, 846 A.2d 75 (Pa. 2004).

"Drowning in Tears." *Fatal Vows*, season 5, episode 12, July 29, 2017.

Dziemianowicz, Joe. "Son Reveals How He Finally Discovered His Father Was a 'Cold, Manipulative Murderer.'" *Oxygen True Crime*, July 23, 2022. https://www.oxygen.com.

Rasmussen, Aaron. "Man Who Strangled Wife in Hot Tub Killed His First Spouse in Bath Four Years Earlier." ID, https://www.investigationdiscovery. com.

State v. Boczkowski, 504 S.E.2d 796 (N.C. App. 1998).

Strong, Marilee. *Erased: Missing Women, Murdered Wives*. San Francisco: Jossey-Bass, 2008.

Thomas, Linn. "Children Gave Information About Mom's Tub Death Four Years Ago." *Greensboro News & Record*, December 26, 1994. https://www. greensboro.com.

Weinstein, Fannie, and Ruth Schumann. *Please Don't Kill Mommy!: The True Story of a Man Who Killed His Wife, Got Away With It, Then Killed Again.* New York: St. Martin's, 2001.

5. SMALL-TOWN CRIMES

Alma Petty

Bost, W.T. "Mrs. Gatlin Will Testify Today in Effort to Clear Herself of Murder Charge." *Greensboro News & Record*, February 18, 1928.

Cannon, J.W. "Local Court Stenographer Seldom Wrong on Verdict." *Greensboro Daily News*, March 18, 1928.

Gardner, D.S. "Admissibility of Confidential Confession to Spiritual Adviser." *North Carolina Law Review* 6, no. 4 (1928): 462. http://scholarship.law.unc.edu.

Greensboro Daily News. "Minister Relates Story of Alleged Confession Made by Mrs. Gatlin." September 4, 1927,

———. "Reidsville Girl Held, Murder Charge." September 4, 1927.

Greensboro News & Record. "Two Organizations Join Their Efforts to Save Mrs. Gatlin from Chair." February 15, 1928.

Link, Phil. *Murder for Breakfast: The True Story of Alma Petty Gatlin and the Preacher Who Betrayed Her.* Asheboro, NC: Down Home Press, 2002.

Ted Kimble

Bartholomew, Nancy. "The Murder Case That Stunned Pleasant Garden." *Greensboro News & Record*, June 24, 2000, updated January 26, 2015. https://greensboro.com.

Chandler-Willis, Lynn. *The Preacher's Son* (originally published as *Unholy Covenant* by Addicus Books). New York: St. Martin's Paperbacks, 2000.

Free Ronnie Kimble website. PWC Consulting (Prevent Wrongful Convictions), published August 15, 2006. http://ronniekimble.com/index.html.

"If I Should Die." *Go Forth and Murder*, season 1, episode 6, first aired May 7, 2020, Investigation Discovery.

6. F<small>AMILY</small> C<small>ONNECTIONS</small>

The Lyerlys and the Data Miner

Bill James Online. "The Lyerly Family." May 10, 2013. https://www.billjamesonline.com.

Hughes, Evan. "Bill James, True-Crime Obsessive, on the Genre's Enduring Importance." *New Yorker*, June 24, 2016. https://www.newyorker.com.

Huler, Scott. *A Delicious Country: Rediscovering the Carolinas Along the Route of John Lawson's 1700 Expedition.* Chapel Hill: University of North Carolina Press, 2019.

James, Bill, and Rachel McCarthy James. *The Man from the Train: The Solving of a Century-Old Serial Killer Mystery.* New York: Scribner, 2017.

NPR. "The Man Behind the 'Moneyball' Sabermetrics." *Talk of the Nation*, September 26, 2011. https://www.npr.org.

Villisca Ax Murder House. https://www.villiscaiowa.com.

Wells, Susan Barringer. *A Game Called Salisbury: The Spinning of a Southern Tragedy*. Np: CreateSpace, 2017.

The Lawson Family Christmas Tragedy

Dietz, Park. "Mass, Serial and Sensational Homicides." *Bulletin of the New York Academy of Medicine* 62, no. 5 (June 1986): 477–91. https://www.ncbi.nlm.nih.gov.

North Carolina Department of Natural and Cultural Resources. "The Story of the Lawson Family." December 25, 2016. https://www.dncr.nc.gov.

Strange Carolinas. "Lawson Family Murders Museum (Madison, NC)." https://www.strangecarolinas.com.

Twin City Sentinel (Winston-Salem). "Suicide Slays Seven." December 26, 1929.

Winston-Salem Journal. "5,000 See Funeral of Eight Slain in Stokes." December 28, 1929.

The Newsom/Lynch Southern Gothic

Associated Press. "Dialect Coach Has Strong Ties to Upcoming Television Movie." *Times-News* (Burlington, NC), December 19, 1993.

Bledsoe, Jerry. "Bitter Blood: A Genealogy of Murder." *Greensboro News & Record* eight-part series, from August 25 to September 1, 1985.

———. *Bitter Blood: A True Story of Southern Family Pride, Madness, and Multiple Murder*. New York: E.P. Dutton, 1988.

Lynch v. NC Department of Justice, et al., 376 S.E.2d 247 (1989).

Moffett, Margaret. "A Day in Infamy: Bitter Blood—The Klenner-Lynch Murders." *Greensboro News & Record*, May 31, 2015.

———. "What We've Lost Is an Awful Lot." *Greensboro News & Record*, June 3, 2015.

The Hallmark Gang

Hornblum, Allen M. *Confessions of a Second Story Man: Junior Kripplebauer and the K&A Gang.* Fort Lee, NJ: Barricade Books, 2006.

Woodall, Martha. "The Hallmark Story." *Greensboro Daily News/Record* six-part series published from April 26 to May 1, 1981.

7. Side Trips, Crime Bits and Oddities

Devil's Tramping Ground

Charlotte Observer. "Signs Now Lead to Mystery." December 9, 1956.

Harden, John. *The Devil's Tramping Ground and Other North Carolina Mystery Stories.* Chapel Hill: University of North Carolina Press, 1949.

Leah, Heather. "'No Human Knows': Devil's Tramping Ground Legend Predates Founding of the United States." WRAL News, October 10, 2020. https://www.wral.com.

UNC-TV Science. "The Devil's Tramping Ground." First aired June 2, 2015. https://video.pbsnc.org.

The No Body Case

DiBiase, Tad. Table of No Body Cases. https://www.nobodycases.com.

Hutson, Jeannine Manning. "1860 Murder Trial Set Precedent." *Greensboro News & Record*, March 4, 1995.

———. "Lexington Prosecutor First to Cite Case." *Greensboro News & Record*, March 4, 1995. https://www.greensboro.com.

State v. Robert T. Williams, 52 NC 446 (1860).

Sullivan, Robert J. *Murders Without Bodies: The Case Files of America's Top "No Body" Homicide Prosecutor.* Irvine, CA: Universal Publishers, 2020.

Henry Alford and His Plea

North Carolina v. Alford. Oral argument, U.S. Sup. Ct., November 17, 1969; published October 14, 1970. https://www.oyez.org/cases/1970/14.

North Carolina v. Alford, 400 U.S. 25 (1970).

Gold

Knapp, Robert F., and Robert M. Topkins. *Gold in History, Geology and Culture: Collected Essays*. Raleigh: North Carolina Division of Archives & History, 2001.

Roberts, Bruce. *The Carolina Gold Rush*. Charlotte, NC: McNally & Loftin, 1972.

Show, Ellen. "The Mint Museum's History Is Women's History." Mint Museum, https://www.mintmuseum.org.

The Million-Dollar Bill

Goessl, Leigh. "Man Tries to Pay for Walmart Purchase with Fake $1 Million Bill." *Winston-Salem Journal*, December 31, 2011. http://www.digitaljournal.com.

Hewlett, Michael. "Charges Dropped Against Man Who Tried to Use $1 Million Bill." *Winston-Salem Journal*, March 2012. https://journalnow.com.

Körner's Folly

Carolina Haints podcast, season 1, episode 9, first aired December 29, 2017.

Sellers, Dan, and Jeffrey Cochran. *Carolina Haints: Ghosts, Folklore, and Mysteries of the Old North State*. Atglen, PA: Schiffer Publishing, 2021.

ABOUT THE AUTHOR

Cathy Pickens, a lawyer and college professor, is a crime fiction writer. Her first novel, *Southern Fried*, won the St. Martin's/Minotaur Best New Traditional Mystery award. The series is now available as the *Blue Ridge Mountain Mysteries* from Joffe Books. She is professor emerita in the McColl School of Business and served as national president of Sisters in Crime and on the boards of Mystery Writers of America and the Mecklenburg Forensic Medicine Program (an evidence collection/preservation training collaborative). She is also the author of *CREATE!* (ICSC Press), offers coaching and workshops on developing the creative process and works with writers on telling their stories.

Her other books from The History Press include:

Charlotte True Crime Stories
True Crime Stories of Eastern North Carolina
Triangle True Crime Stories
True Crime Stories of Upstate South Carolina
True Crime Stories of Western North Carolina
True Crime Stories of South Carolina's Midlands
Charleston Mysteries

Visit us at
www.historypress.com
....